A HISTORY OF BRITAIN
Book VIII

The Second World War and its Aftermath, 1939-1951

This eighth volume in the evolving series charts Britain's varying fortunes in the worldwide theatre of war against Nazi Germany, Fascist Italy and imperial Japan. The Second World War evoked a desire for change, leading to Labour's landslide victory in 1945 and the creation of the Welfare State, the National Health Service and widespread nationalization of industry and services. Europe was divided between the East, ruled by the (communist) Soviet Union and the (US-shielded) West. The independence of the Indian sub-continent began the transformation of the Empire into the British Commonwealth. The war and the period of Labour rule (1945-51) that followed constitute a watershed in British history.

EH Carter was Chief Inspector of Schools in the 1930s and '40s. **RAF Mears** taught history at Warwick School between 1923 and 1933.

David Evans, who edits the restored series, is an historian and former Head of History at Eton College.

PUBLICATION SCHEDULE

A HISTORY OF BRITAIN

The Second World War and its Aftermath

♦

1939-1951

by

EH Carter & RAF Mears

edited and updated by

David Evans

STACEY
INTERNATIONAL

A HISTORY OF BRITAIN
The Second World War and its Aftermath, 1939-1951

STACEY INTERNATIONAL
128 Kensington Church Street
London W8 4BH
Tel: +44 (0)20 7221 7166; Fax: +44 (0)20 7792 9288
Email: info@stacey-international.co.uk
www.stacey-international.co.uk

ISBN: 978 1906768492

This version © Stacey International 2011

Original edition published in 1937 by The Clarendon Press

1 3 5 7 9 0 8 6 4 2

Printed in the United Kingdom

The Publishers of this edition of *The History of Britain*, revised by David Evans (formerly Head of History, Eton College), give wholehearted acknowledgment to the original work of the late E H Carter (sometime Chief Examiner in History, Board of Education, and H M Inspector of Schools) and R A F Mears (former Senior History Master, Warwick School), who died respectively in 1954 and 1940. The Publishers declare that prolonged endeavours devoted to tracing whether rights to the work of these two distinguished scholars rested with any successors or assigns have been made.

Maps by Amber Sheers

CIP Data: A catalogue record for this book is available from the British Library

Contents

List of Illustrations

Maps

Glossary

Appeasement	policy of making concessions in the hope of satisfying a ruler or power
Balance of payments	the difference between a country's spending on imports and earnings on exports
Capitalism	economic system in which most industry is run by private firms
Consensus	very widespread agreement
Dominion	self-governing state within the British Commonwealth
Duce	Leader (Italian), the title assumed by Mussolini
Fascist	connected with Mussolini's regime; often used to describe any authoritarian, non-Communist regime
Federal	belonging to country composed of several states
Führer	Leader (German), title assumed by Hitler
Inflation	rising prices
Laisser (OR laissez) faire	avoidance of government interference in economic and social matters
Lebensraum	living space, land desired by Hitler to expand German power
Luftwaffe	German air force
Modernism	movement in the arts rejecting traditional styles
Monotheism	belief in one God
Nationalization	takeover of an industry by the state
Pacifist	someone who rejects war as a method of solving disputes
Proletariat	the working class
Reich	the German state or Empire
The Third Reich	Hitler's regime
Status quo	the existing state of affairs
U-boat	German submarine
Wehrmacht	German armed forces

Whip	party official who ensures that MPs vote in the Commons as directed by the party leaders
Zionism	a movement among Jews to found a Jewish state in the Holy Land

Note on Money

In this period, Britain's currency was not decimalized. There were 12 old pennies to the shilling and 20 shillings to the pound sterling. (Hence there were 240 pence to the pound.) The old penny was abbreviated as *d*, the shilling as *s* and the pound as £.

DATE SUMMARY: Second World War 1939-45

WAR IN EUROPE	MIDDLE EAST	NAVAL AND FAR EAST
	1939	
Sept. B.E.F. holds Belgian frontier		Sept. ⚔ Battle of the Atlantic begins
	1940	
Apr. Germany invades Norway and Denmark.		
May. Germany invades Holland, Belgium, France		
June. Fall of France	June. Italy declares was on Allies	
Aug. ⚔ Battle of Britain		
	1941	
	Feb. Cyrenaica overrun by British	
	Apr. Germans invade Greece, Cyrenaica	
	May. Abyssinia freed	May. *Bismark* sunk
June. German invasion of Russia		
	July. British & Free French in Syria	
	Dec. British reoccupy Cyrenaica	Dec. Japan and U.S.A. enter war
	1942	
		Feb.-May. Loss of Dutch East Indies, Burma, Philippines
	July. Rommel 80 miles from Alexandria	July. Austrian advance in New Guinea
	Oct. ⚔ Battle of El Alamein	
Dec. Battle Stalingrad	Nov. American and British landings at Algiers	
	1943	
General Russian advance throughout the year	May. All Axis troops in Africa surrender	
	July. Allied landings in Sicily and S. Italy	
	1944	
June. British and American landings in Normandy		June. British advances into Burma
Aug. Paris liberated		
Sept. Belgium liberated		
⚔ Arnhem (Holland)		
Oct. Russians cross German frontier		Oct. Greece liberated
	1945	
Feb. Allies cross the Rhine		
Russians cross the Oder		

7th May 1945, unconditional surrender of Germany

June. Rangoon recaptured
American occupation of Okinawa
Aug. Hiroshima and Nagasaki – atomic bomb

14 August 1945, unconditional surrender of Japan

10

INTRODUCTION

THE slaughter of trench warfare between 1914 and 1918 had produced in inter-war Britain a revulsion against war and against everything that was alleged to cause war, such as great armaments, secret diplomacy and military ententes with other powers. The jingoism (or noisy patriotism) of the Edwardian period was out of fashion, condemned for leading to the bloodbath in Flanders, and in 1933 in the Oxford Union the resolution that 'this House will not fight for King and Country' was carried by a substantial majority. The hope of many people was that in the League of Nations rational modern man had invented a mechanism for the resolution of disputes that might enable humanity to avoid armed conflict in future. Few statesmen believed in the efficacy of the League, though they found it expedient on occasion to pretend that they did. Nonetheless, a statesman such as Neville Chamberlain, who, as Prime Minister, took charge of Britain's foreign policy from 1937, found it hard to believe that international disputes could not be settled by reasonable discussion and compromise. This was the assumption behind his policy of appeasement, which culminated in his approaches to Adolf Hitler over the Czech crisis in the autumn of 1938. He got Hitler to subscribe to the same view of how disputes should be settled in the Anglo-German Declaration, signed before the Prime Minister left Munich in 1938. That Chamberlain was indulging in wishful thinking when he put trust in the Declaration became apparent in March 1939, when Hitler flouted the Treaty of Munich by occupying Prague and the Czech lands without any reference whatever to Britain and France.

After the occupation of Prague, Chamberlain had not yet reconciled himself to war, but the episode confirmed a shift in his government's policy that was already taking place. The emphasis was increasingly on deterring Hitler from making further unilateral changes in Europe. The British government made it much clearer than it had ever been before what would not be tolerated. It also sought to make clear what Hitler would face by way of military and economic consequences should he flout the British prohibitions. Deterrence could be made convincing only if rearmament was undertaken at full speed. At last, Britain began to emulate Germany in the proportion of its national wealth devoted to its military forces. Britain once again planned to send a force to assist France, should it be attacked. While hoping for peace, then, Chamberlain found himself implicitly threatening war.

By this time public opinion was no longer pacifist. The Nazi regime was easy to dislike. The details of the attacks on the Jews during the Night of Broken Glass (Kristallnacht) in November 1938, so called because the windows of Jewish-owned shops were smashed, were well known in Britain. Labour and the British left were well aware that, apart from the Jews, Hitler's chief victims had been trade unionists, socialists and Communists. They knew too that he had joined with other dictators such as Mussolini to help crush the forces of democracy in the Spanish Civil War. Men on the left joined with Conservative critics of the government such as Winston Churchill to urge resistance to the Nazi threat to Europe. No one in 1939 would thank God for matching them with the hour of conflict, as Rupert Brooke had in his poem of 1914. War was not welcomed, but people were increasingly resigned to it as necessary to rid the world of an evil and aggressive regime.

The object of Chamberlain's government was not to rid the world of evil, but to preserve the principle that Europe's future should be determined not by one dominant power, but by discussion among its great powers. Germany was not the only threat to this principle. The Soviet Union was, potentially at least, a state of such power that it might loom over Europe and attempt to control its destiny. In the 1930s Joseph Stalin had attempted to realize the huge potential of his state by launching a programme of rapid industrialization. His concentration on heavy industry, as opposed to consumer goods industries, made it obvious that his primary aim was to increase the military power of the Soviet Union, an aim that became increasingly explicit as his Five Year Plans succeeded one another. Mistrust of the Soviet colossus is a major reason why Chamberlain much preferred to solve Europe's problems without the involvement of Stalin. The Soviet dictator was at no point consulted as the Czech crisis developed in 1938. The other potential controller of Europe's destiny was the United States of America. Chamberlain could not avoid some dependence on the USA. Britain and France would need access to American arms and raw materials should the worst happen and by 1939, at the price of a confrontation with Congress, President Roosevelt had granted them such access. That the USA was unwilling to do more suited Chamberlain well. He preferred not to have the USA in a position where it might try to determine Europe's future, perhaps with more persistence and success than in 1918-19. Yet war with Germany was risky. A war in which Germany and the Anglo-French alliance exhausted each other might lead to a situation in which the USSR or the USA or both called the shots in Europe.

The government was only too aware that saving Europe from the Third Reich could easily prove fatal to the British Empire. It was not that Britain expected to lose the war against Germany. Chamberlain expected a long war of at least three years, but he believed that in the end Britain would win. What he feared was that Britain's other enemies would seize the opportunity presented by the country's involvement in Europe to attack the Empire elsewhere. This was a major reason why he had tried so hard to avoid a war with Germany by means of appeasement and deterrence. One of these other enemies was Benito Mussolini, the Italian dictator, who seemed able to disrupt British communications through the Mediterranean and so to undermine the entire British position in the Middle East. In the Far East, Japan had since 1937 been involved in a war for the control of eastern China. Britain had built Singapore into a major naval base, but lacked the modern ships to send there. Should Singapore fall, the entire Empire in Asia and Australasia would be in mortal peril. In fact, in 1939 neither Mussolini nor Japan was ready to support Hitler by attacking the British Empire, but the danger that they would do so as soon as Britain suffered any serious reverse remained.

It became clear in 1939 that the self-governing Dominions of the British Empire would support Britain in its war with Germany, with the exception of the Irish Free State, where de Valera proclaimed the country's neutrality. Elsewhere, it was possible that war might strain the bonds of empire to breaking point. Britain's quarrel with Germany was not one that Egyptians or Indians would necessarily feel concerned them. German, Italian or Japanese expansionists might find an audience for offers of freedom from the British yoke. Resentment of British rule was certain to be heightened by demands for men and materials and by the stationing of troops in strategically vital areas of the Middle East. Even if Britain somehow maintained its hold over such countries as Egypt and India till the end of the war, it was unlikely that the Empire could survive into a post-war world. War might leave Britain deeply in debt to the USA, which was not sympathetic towards European imperialisms.

Another great war was likely to have consequences for Britain's internal development as well as for its Empire. The First World War had produced a huge stride towards greater democracy in the form of the Representation of the People Act of 1918 and promises to build 'homes fit for heroes'. The amount of social reform carried out had in the end been disappointing, but that very disappointment would produce a determination that after a second great war things would be different. During a great war the government had to direct the entire economy in order to give priority to the achievement of victory. The economist JM Keynes was enlisted to advise the government on how to proceed. But Keynes had ideas for peacetime government too, especially about the way to eliminate unemployment, that great social evil of the inter-war years. One of the results of the war was likely to be a greater faith in the government's ability to shape the economy and society by means of economic planning. War also meant the adoption of measures to assist the vulnerable in society and to enforce a degree of social justice, by means of rationing, for example. Many steps towards these goals had already been taken before 1939, but war would produce a demand for a more comprehensive system, for what came to be known as the welfare state. Before 1939 social reform had been impeded by reluctance to raise taxes to pay for it, but war would accustom people to paying higher taxes.

In 1939 Britain stood on the threshold of another great war. The war would transform its international position and have a major impact on the Empire. The war was followed by a period of internal change and reform. The Second World War, its effects on Britain and the changes carried out in its aftermath are the subject of this book.

I

THE OUTBREAK OF
THE SECOND WORLD WAR

1. The Issue of Poland

Hitler comes to power 1933

ADOLF Hitler came to power in Germany in 1933. In the course of about eighteen months he established himself as dictator of what he called the Third Reich. His political party, the National Socialist or Nazi party, was the only party allowed. The Nazis aimed to bind all inhabitants of Germany together in a united national community, which, they believed, could happen only if everyone who lived in Germany was ethnically German. Hence no Jew or gypsy had any place in Nazi Germany. People of these races were deprived of rights and then of their livelihoods, and finally every effort was made to get rid of them by emigration. In Hitler's mind, racial unity was a pre-condition for a new and this time successful bid to establish Germany as a world power. This was the essential purpose of his regime, but it was several years before this became clear. Hitler had first to end the restrictions imposed upon Germany by the Treaty of Versailles, a goal finally accomplished when Austria was swallowed up in defiance of the Treaty in March 1938 (Anschluss). The undermining of Czechoslovakia, which followed, could be justified on the grounds that the three million ethnic Germans who lived there, mostly in the border area known as the Sudetenland, deserved the right to be included in the German Reich if they wished. The issue of the Germans within Czechoslovakia was resolved at the Munich Conference on 1 October, 1938. Hitler's next step was neither a removal of an artificial restriction imposed at Versailles, nor a righting of wrongs done to ethnic Germans. On 15 March 1939, German forces occupied Prague and the next day the Czech lands were declared a protectorate of Germany. Hitler had unilaterally revised

Racial and anti-semitic policies

Anschluss March 1938

Annexation of Czech-oslovakia March 1939

16

Europe in the First Months of the War, 1939-40

the Munich Agreement, which he himself had made with Britain and France less than six months previously. In doing so, he showed that the Anglo-German Declaration pledging the two countries to consult in future on important European issues was worthless. The three flights to Germany of the British Prime Minister Neville Chamberlain in the early autumn of 1938 had not brought 'peace with honour' after all.

There were many rumours about where Hitler might strike next, but it was obvious that at some stage soon he would want to settle the question of Poland. The very existence of an independent Poland was resented by many Germans, particularly since at Versailles Poland had been given a corridor to the sea which split East Prussia from the rest of Germany and contained a large German minority of about 800,000 people. For Poland's benefit, in order to allow the country a port, the

THE MUNICH CONFERENCE, 1 OCTOBER 1938

Danzig and the Polish Corridor

wholly German port of Danzig had been given a special status. Though it was allowed internal self-government, it was not joined to the Reich and its foreign affairs and customs regulations were run by the Poles. The German case for some changes in the settlement arrived at after the First World War was a strong one. Achieving improvements in Germany's favour would also enhance Hitler's popularity. Of all his foreign policies, none had aroused so much domestic criticism as his Non-Aggression Pact with Poland of 1934. Nonetheless, when he raised the issues of Danzig and the Corridor with the Polish government in the winter of 1938-9, it was not because these issues mattered greatly in themselves. As the Poles realized, Hitler expected the Poles to give way on these matters as a sign of their general willingness to accept the reality of German control over eastern Europe in the wake of his coup in Prague. Hitler needed Poland to accept satellite status. If it did, then he would be able to strike east through it at the Soviet Union, the scenario envisaged in his

Non-Aggression Pact 1934

book of the mid-1920s, *Mein Kampf* (My Struggle). Alternatively, he could decide to strike west at Britain and France, without having to *Mein Kampf* worry about a possible stab in the back from the Poles.

Even before Hitler's coup in Prague, the Poles had made clear to the Germans their absolute refusal to give way to German demands as the Czechs had done. There was something magnificent about their courage, foolhardy though it was. Poland had none of the natural defences which the Czechs had possessed until they gave them away at Munich. It was on bad terms with its other powerful neighbour, the USSR, still resentful of the way that Poland had taken advantage of Soviet weakness in 1920-21 to push its frontier eastwards. The Poles' chances of preventing the Germans from defeating and destroying their state if war broke out were slim.

What made the quarrel between Germany and Poland important was an accident of timing. The dispute was simmering at the very moment when Hitler's forces invaded Prague and thereby rendered unconvincing all Chamberlain's assertions about what he had achieved at Munich. The British government was in danger of being overthrown in the House of Commons. It had to show its willingness to stand up to Hitler. The method it chose was to offer Britain to Poland a public guarantee of its independence on 31 March, guarantees 1939. This guarantee, in which France joined, was followed a Polish indepen- fortnight later by guarantees to Greece and Romania. The guarantee dence March given to Poland was a guarantee of the country's independence, not 1939 of its territorial integrity: it did not rule out possible concessions to Germany over Danzig or the Corridor. What was ruled out, Chamberlain explained, was 'forcible aggression'. This meant that the Poles, unlike the Czechs the year before, could not be compelled to negotiate under threat. The chances of their making concessions to Hitler, never good, were now negligible. Yet Hitler was determined to solve his Polish problem and solve it soon. In April he issued the directive for Operation White, war against Poland, Operation though he emphasized that the country must first be isolated. The White guarantee to Poland was important, because, against Hitler's expectations, it made the isolation of Poland impossible to achieve.

The British and French governments fervently hoped that their guarantee to Poland would deter Hitler from attacking it. Yet they had to reckon with the possibility that Hitler would not be deterred from attacking Poland and that they would therefore have to back up their guarantee by going to war against an aggressive Germany. Their policy risked war. They would hardly have pursued it had they not believed in their chances of success in a war. By 1939 their situation looked much better than it had in 1938. Both Britain and France were having some success in rallying their empires. The American President, Roosevelt, was proving, in Chamberlain's words, 'wary but helpful'. The French and British needed to use the US as their arsenal, and from the end of 1938 Roosevelt began to open to the Western powers the resources of the American aircraft industry. The rearmament programmes of Britain and France had by 1939 made the two powers much more of a match for Germany than they had been at the time of the Czech crisis. By the summer of 1939 their tank and aircraft production was known through military intelligence to exceed that of Germany. British air defences, based on radar and fast monoplane fighters, were almost ready. The British and French both believed that continued massive rearmament would begin to overstrain their economies in 1940 or so. If a war against Hitler had to be fought, then 1939 might be the optimum year in which to launch it.

British & French rearmament

What the Allies lacked was any credible plan for assisting the Poles. General Gamelin had reckoned in 1938 that France would need two years of preparation before it could mount a successful offensive against Germany. In 1939 France would still have to rely on the strong fortifications of the Maginot Line to keep the Germans at bay while preparations for an offensive were completed. The fighting of the Poles might help to buy time for France and Britain, but there was little prospect of a vigorous attack on Germany, which was the only way in which the Allies could help the Poles. For the Allies, the issue

Maginot Line

was not really Poland. Like Czechoslovakia, it was 'a far-away country' inhabited by a 'people of whom we know nothing'.* There was nothing very endearing about the Poles, whose government was authoritarian and anti-semitic and had been only too eager to profit from the downfall of neighbouring Czechoslovakia. If Britain and France went to war, it would not be out of love for the Poles, but for the principle that they were great powers which must be consulted over changes to the European political system. Hitler's demands on Poland simply furnished a convenient test case.

2. The Nazi-Soviet Pact

Since the crisis over Czechoslovakia in September 1938, it had been clear that Hitler could not count on the neutrality of Britain, as he had earlier hoped. If Britain insisted on limiting Germany's freedom of action, then an Anglo-German war was inevitable. Given that Britain had an ally in France, reserves of manpower and raw materials in its Empire and probable access to America's almost limitless resources, war with Britain was a daunting prospect. Soon after Munich, therefore, the German regime adopted a programme which involved a tripling of armaments production by the early 1940s. Yet it rapidly became clear that the programme was entirely unrealistic. Germany had to import huge quantities of raw materials: iron ore, non-ferrous metals and oil, for example. To procure these essentials some of Germany's industrial effort had to be devoted to making articles for export, which limited the proportion of Germany's productive capacity that could be geared to the production of armaments. Instead of the wished-for expansion, the targets for ammunition, tanks and aircraft had to be scaled back in the course of 1939. This was not all that went

German rearmament

---

* This is what Chamberlain had said about the Czechs at the height of the crisis in September 1938.

wrong for Hitler. He needed Japan to attack British colonial possessions in the Far East in order to divert Britain's attention and resources away from Europe. The Japanese, however, refused to play Hitler's game. They had enough on their hands with a war in China and a stand-off against the Soviet Union on its far eastern borders. Mussolini was eager enough to sign the Pact of Steel in May 1939. Thereby he showed that he was not available as a possible ally of Britain and France and pledged himself to help Germany unconditionally in the event of war. Yet at the same time he made it clear that Italy would not be ready for war for some years to come: 1943 was the date he mentioned. The Germans could clearly not place much reliance on the Duce to tie down Britain in the defence of the Middle East. He did indeed let them down when war broke out in September 1939.

Pact of Steel
May 1939

At the heart of Hitler's difficulties was the fact that Germany was only a middle-sized European state that was pitting itself against two other middle-sized states which, through their empires and links with the USA, could draw on the resources of the world beyond Europe. Not only that, but Britain's navy would enable it to cut Germany off almost entirely from the extra-European world. This is what had happened, Hitler believed, in the First World War, when Britain had imposed its blockade. He thought that it had been a fatal error of Imperial Germany that it had antagonized Britain, but he had gone on to make the same mistake. There was, however, an important difference between the situation in 1939 and that of 1914. In 1914 the western powers had encircled Germany through their alliance with Russia. In early 1939 the USSR was not yet committed to either side.

In 1939 the western powers and the Nazi regime both sought the friendship of the USSR. The spectacle of conflict among the capitalist powers was not in the least surprising to Stalin, since such conflict had been predicted by Lenin, the founder and theorist of Soviet Communism. Neither side could be trusted, for capitalist states inevitably sought to destroy states which represented a different social and economic system. Hitler had never made any secret of his detestation of Bolshevism and his resolve to destroy it. The western powers were less forthright, but Stalin suspected that they hoped to embroil him with Hitler with the aim of weakening both the USSR and Germany. The situation contained dangers for the USSR, then, but it also presented opportunities. Stalin could take advantage of the conflict to charge a high price for his friendship. The contest for Stalin's favour was not one which the western powers had any chance of winning.

The western leaders, and especially the British ones, undertook the negotiations with Stalin with a distinct lack of enthusiasm. 'I must confess the most profound distrust of Russia, and I distrust her motives, which seem to me to have little connection with our idea of liberty, and to be concerned only with getting everyone else by the ears,' wrote Chamberlain. The British military were sceptical about the military value of a Soviet alliance after Stalin's purges of the high command of his armed forces in 1937-8. To some extent the negotiations were pursued to keep the trade unions and the left happy. The French were much keener: co-operation with Russia had a long history dating back to the 1890s. Stalin's decision, however, was not likely to be determined by French enthusiasm or British lack of it. He was concerned with concrete gains for the USSR, but in this respect Britain and France had nothing to offer. Concrete gains for the Soviets could come only at the expense of the smaller states between Germany and the USSR, but these were the very states whose friendship the West had been seeking and whose independence they claimed to uphold against Germany. The Polish guarantee of March 1939 was incompatible with the Soviet alliance, though this was not at once clear either to Stalin or the West. Perhaps the most important gain which Stalin hoped for was a swathe of eastern Poland which the Poles had seized in the war of 1920-21, but plainly this was not on offer from the West. Still more important, if they were to be military allies against Germany, the Soviets would need access to its frontiers. That meant

British distrust of Stalin

Russian territorial ambitions in Poland

crossing Poland, but the Poles refused access, fearing, justifiably enough, that once Soviet troops were in the country, it would prove impossible to get them out again. From the western point of view, the chief aim of their talks with Stalin was to put pressure on Hitler and persuade him that his position was not strong enough to permit him to risk war. Stalin had no interest in playing this role, which threatened to bring Hitler in his direction if Hitler risked war after all, while offering him no compensating gains whatever.

A Soviet alliance with the Nazis seemed even more improbable than one with the West. A large part of Hitler's appeal to his countrymen had been his claim to be the most effective defender of Germany against Communism. In *Mein Kampf* he had identified Russia as the target of German expansion. Italy and Japan had in 1936-7 been brought into an alliance with Germany directed against Communism. Yet in 1939 his anti-Communist allies were about to let him down. Hitler was desperate. By the summer of 1939 he urgently needed the Soviet alliance. Securing it might finally make the British realize the hopelessness of Poland's position and procure their abstention from the coming war against Poland. This seemed all the more likely because the weapon they were counting on in any conflict against Germany would no longer work. When Hitler did secure an alliance with Stalin, he boasted to his generals that Germany now had nothing to fear from a blockade. An agreement with the Soviets outflanked the British blockade by giving him access to the raw materials of the Soviet Union itself and access via the USSR to the raw materials of Asia beyond it.

Molotov-
Ribbentrop
Pact
August 1939

Hitler had, of course, to pay a price for his pact with the Soviet Union, negotiated by Foreign Minister Ribbentrop and his Soviet opposite number Molotov. Actually, it was the small states of eastern Europe which paid the price. Unlike the West, Hitler could freely give away Poland's territory: Stalin was to have the eastern part of the country to right at last the wrong done to the USSR in the Russo-Polish War of 1920. Hitler was prepared too to give Stalin a free hand in Finland, Estonia and Latvia, gains which greatly enhanced the security of Leningrad. Further south, Soviet interest in Bessarabia, an eastern province of Romania, was recognised. In return for all these prizes Stalin had only to promise neutrality in any war in which Germany was involved. He was well aware that his promise involved him in no danger of attack from Britain and France. He had bought valuable time to reorganize his armed forces after the terrible bloodletting of 1937. Not that he supposed that the respite would last for ever: war with the capitalist state of Germany was inevitable. He could count, however, on Germany's being much weakened by its forthcoming struggle with the West.

Stalin gains from non-aggression treaty

3. War over Poland

If the position of Poland had been weak before the signature of the Nazi-Soviet Pact on 24 August 1939, afterwards it was totally hopeless. Hitler seems to have expected that Britain would abandon its commitment to the Poles. He told his generals just before the Pact was signed: 'War between Poland and Germany will remain localized … England and France will make threats, but will not declare war.' In fact, news of the Pact failed to have the impact on the West that Hitler anticipated. There had never been any plans to fight in eastern Europe and it had never been expected that Stalin would give worthwhile military support there. Insofar as the Pact left Stalin free to fight the Japanese on his far eastern border, it helped Britain by ensuring that the Japanese would not dare to take on more enemies by attacking the British Empire in the Far East.

Britain confounded Hitler's expectations by signing an alliance with Poland on 25 August and he put back the invasion by a few days in order to make another attempt to isolate the Poles. The British and French urged the Poles to make reasonable concessions to Germany over Danzig and the Corridor, but Hitler was not angling for a peaceful solution. He was simply attempting to split Poland from its

Britain signs alliance with Poland

western supporters. He was determined to show who was boss in eastern Europe by crushing the Poles by force. The West was determined to deny him the power to re-model Europe at will. The aims of Hitler and the western leaders were incompatible.

Though Hitler hoped for western neutrality till the last minute, he was not counting on it. It would have been convenient to isolate Poland, since a determined assault by the French against the western frontier of Germany while the bulk of German forces were tied down in Poland could have been fatal. Yet a showdown with the western powers in the near future seemed to Hitler to be in Germany's best interests. Now that the West was seriously rearming, it was likely to outspend Germany and open up an increasing lead in the quantity of its armaments. If President Roosevelt could once get rid of the restrictions of the Neutrality Acts and aid the western powers as much as he clearly wanted, then Germany might find itself wholly outclassed. Time was against the Germans and though they were not ready for a great war, their position relative to the other powers was better than it would be in the future. Their early rearmament had given them a lead in the number of their aeroplanes and the combat-readiness of their air and land forces. The construction of the Westwall, a defensive system of bunkers and gun emplacements plugging the gap between the Rhine and Moselle, ensured that the French would not enjoy a promenade into Germany. When talking to his generals in August 1939 of the forthcoming war, Hitler said: 'We have nothing to lose; we have everything to gain. Because of our restrictions our economic situation is such that we can only hold out for a few more years…We must act.'

On 1 September 1939 Hitler did act by unleashing his troops on the Poles. Two days later Britain and France declared war on Germany. Yet though Hitler had been wrong to suppose that the West would not declare war, he was largely right in supposing that Britain and France would not actually make war for Poland. The slow French mobilization system and their insistence that nothing could be done

Germany strengthens defences

Germany invades Poland 1 Sept. 1939

without an artillery bombardment from heavy guns that had to be brought out of storage delayed any serious attack for two weeks. By then it was all up with Poland and the forces of the western powers remained on the defensive.

Poland had proved totally helpless against German armed might. Its strategic position was very weak: the Germans were able to attack from three sides, the west, East Prussia and the Czech lands and Slovakia. The Poles were unable to concentrate their forces effectively and their armies became cut off from one another. The Poles raised as many men as the Germans, about one and a half million, but the Germans were better equipped with tanks and motorized transport. It was above all German air power which won the war. The Germans had far more aircraft of far higher quality. Within days the Polish air force had been driven from the skies and the Germans were able to bomb arms factories, strafe Polish troops and terrorize Polish cities with impunity, since the Poles had only 100 anti-aircraft guns for the entire country. By the time the Red Army moved into eastern Poland to claim the Soviet share of the country, on 17 September, Poland had already effectively been defeated, though the last large force did not give up the fight until early October.

The German campaign against Poland is usually described as the first example of *Blitzkrieg* or lightning war, a type of warfare characterized by the use of tanks and aircraft and designed to overwhelm the enemy within days. Unlike the static warfare of the First World War, in which the combatants aimed to wear each other down, this was mobile warfare which sought a rapid and decisive result. Yet the German forces that achieved this result had striking weaknesses. German success was only to be expected against so weak an opponent and was attained by an army that was far from fully modernized. Most of the infantry still moved on foot and artillery and equipment was pulled along by over 300,000 horses. The price the Germans paid for their victory was not altogether negligible and revealed serious shortcomings in their military machine. In under a

Blitzkrieg

German
military
weaknesses

month of fighting, a quarter of the initial force of tanks had broken down or been destroyed. Huge numbers of vehicles had been knocked out and the loss of aircraft had been considerable. Success against Britain and France was most certainly not guaranteed and the leaders of the Wehrmacht (the German armed forces) viewed the coming struggle with concern.

II

DISASTER: THE BATTLE OF FRANCE

1. The Phoney War

BETWEEN the defeat of Poland and the spring of 1940 there was so little military action that the American press dubbed these months the 'Phoney War'. There was considerable activity in Britain itself, mainly concerned with preparations against the expected bombing offensive. Anderson shelters, named after the minister responsible, were distributed and erected in people's gardens. These were air raid shelters made of curved sections of corrugated steel bolted together and sunk into the ground over a hole four feet deep and ten feet wide. With soil loaded on top, they were reckoned to give protection against all but a direct hit. Unfortunately, they tended to fill up with muddy water. In their homes, people webbed their windows with tape to prevent injuries from flying glass. Heavy dark curtains had to be hung to prevent the light escaping. At night the blackout was strictly enforced by those appointed as ARP (Air Raid Protection) wardens. Cars had to travel with hoods over their headlamps. The appearance of London changed as Oxford Street stores boarded up their windows and sandbags were stacked against doors and windows as protection against blast. Works of art and irreplaceable documents were moved to places of safety, while half the children of London were moved into the countryside. All these precautions turned out to be premature. The Luftwaffe's bombers lacked the range to launch a bombing offensive against England. They could become a real threat only when they acquired bases closer to their targets. By that time many of those evacuated had gone back home.

Meanwhile, the armed forces of France and Britain remained on the defensive. Their governments expected a long war in which their chances of success were thought to be greater. As they had hoped,

Anderson Shelters

Blackout

Evacuation of children

29

Hitler's attack on Poland affected opinion in America and President
Roosevelt was able to secure the revision of the Neutrality Acts and
open up the industrial capacity of the USA to the western Allies,
though they had to pay for what they took under the Cash and Carry
scheme. By the summer of 1940 they had on order more than 10,000
military aircraft, to be delivered by the end of 1941, the equivalent of
a whole year's production by the Reich. While the West could look
forward to this plenty, the armed forces of the Reich faced starvation.
The Reich had to make its own weaponry, but the imports necessary
for doing so were reduced by 80 per cent thanks to the British
blockade. The agreements with Stalin could help the Reich to survive
this squeeze, but Stalin's help did not come free. In return the Reich
had to supply him with equipment. In this bleak situation, Colonel
Thomas, the German Army's chief economics expert, advised a policy
of careful conservation of the stock of raw materials in order to eke
them out over three years. This was exactly what the leaders of the
West expected the Germans to do. If they had done so, no doubt the
balance would gradually have tilted towards the West and maybe the
West's hope that Hitler would finally be discredited and fall from
power would have been realized. Essentially, this scenario would have
been a repetition of the First World War. This was exactly what Hitler
was determined to prevent.

Hitler insisted that the build-up of armaments must be put into
over-drive, regardless of the consequences for the sustainability in the
long term of the German war effort. The German position was too
weak for Germany to allow itself to proceed following the conventional
logic of men like Colonel Thomas. Germany's only hope was to stake
all on a gambler's throw against the western powers, and the gamble
had to be undertaken as soon as possible, before the odds against
success lengthened too greatly. As early as 27 September 1939, Hitler
said to his chief commanders: 'The "time-factor" is in general not on
our side, unless we exploit it to the utmost. Economic means of the
other side are stronger.' This consideration led the Führer to order an

Revision of Neutrality Acts (margin note)

Hitler's plans for an early strike (margin note)

attack as early as 12 November 1939. The generals were appalled, but the convincing lists of difficulties that they produced, such as the woeful state of the Panzer (tank) forces after the Polish campaign, simply threw Hitler into a towering rage. In the end, the weather came to their aid, convincing even Hitler that he would have to wait for a season when the Luftwaffe would be able to provide adequate air cover for a strike against the West.

German offensive delayed

Had Hitler launched his forces against the West in late 1939, then they would have followed a plan produced in October 1939 that was very similar to the Schlieffen Plan of 1914. The main thrust would have been through central Belgium, while a secondary attack would have proceeded through the woods and hills of the Ardennes. All the tanks would have been attached to the main attack, since the narrow and twisting roads of the Ardennes were regarded as too difficult for them. The goal of the attack was the capture of the Channel ports, which would make possible an air assault on England. There were problems with this plan. It accorded exactly with the expectations of the western commanders, who were only too anxious to re-fight the war of 1914. It was also unlikely to produce a decisive result. The German critic of the plan, General Erich von Manstein, thought it likely to produce a stalemate on the Somme. Nor did it accord with Hitler's thinking about the purposes of the campaign, which went beyond the mere capture of the Channel ports to the entire overthrow of the French army. Anything less would bring on the war of attrition which Germany could not win. It was, however, an accident that led to the abandonment of the plan.

Drawbacks of Germany's offensive plans

On 10 January 1940 an officer carrying the operational plan for the attack in the West was forced to land in Belgium and the plan ended up in western hands. Though the Germans did not know what had happened to the plan, they were bound to assume the worst and Hitler decided that it must be changed. Manstein had already produced an alternative, which had been judged too risky. In the new circumstances, however, this plan was reconsidered and under

Manstein
Plan adopted

pressure from Hitler the High Command finally adopted it. In this plan, the attack through the Ardennes became the major one, involving 45 crack divisions. The attack further north was secondary, to be carried out by 29 divisions, designed to absorb the attention of the British and French troops in central Belgium. The Allies obliged the Germans by adopting Gamelin's Plan D, which placed the British and the pick of the French troops on the Allied left in central Belgium. If the thrust through the Ardennes succeeded, then the Germans in that sector would have the chance to cut through France to the Channel coast and encircle the Anglo-French armies in Belgium, compelling their surrender.

Before the Germans could put their plan into action, Hitler decided to intervene in Scandinavia.

2. The Norwegian Campaign

Scandinavian
iron ore
vital to
Germany

British
intervention
in Narvik
and
Norwegian
waters

Scandinavia mattered to the Germans as the place from which much of their iron ore came. The Germans imported more than half of the iron ore they used and over 80 per cent of the imports came from Sweden. Should the ore supplies have been interrupted, German arms production would soon have been subjected to a drastic squeeze. The Swedes had no intention of displeasing Nazi Germany, however, especially as they depended on the Reich for their supplies of coal. The Germans were less certain that they could depend upon Norway. In the winter months the ore was shipped to Germany through the Norwegian port of Narvik. Aware of this, Churchill, who at the outbreak of the war with Germany had been appointed to the Admiralty, had agitated for some time for British intervention in Norway, where it seemed that British seapower could be decisive, but many in the government were more reluctant to violate Norwegian neutrality than he was. Finally, it was agreed to place mines in Norwegian waters and to land troops at Narvik early in April 1940. By then the Germans had also decided to act.

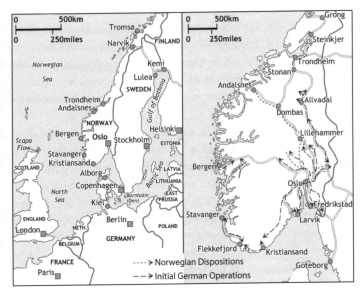

THE INVASION OF NORWAY, APRIL 1940

For a long time Hitler insisted that Norwegian neutrality served German interests best, but early in 1940 he was visited by Vidkun Quisling, leader of the Norwegian Fascist party, who persuaded him that the British threat was real. Hitler proceeded to issue the order for the 'Weser Exercise' which involved the conquest of Denmark and Norway. In the dark hours of 9 April Denmark was attacked by land, sea and air. Complete surprise was achieved and resistance ceased after less than two hours. At the same time, a parachute battalion took over the principal airfields of Norway, while a total of 10,000 troops were landed at the chief ports from Oslo to Narvik. Norwegian resistance was largely ineffective, since mobilization was ordered far too late and was disrupted by rapid German action. The British fleet was already pursuing its plans in Norwegian waters. It achieved some success against the German Navy, but it was too far offshore and too hampered by the haze and indented coastline to prevent the German

Vidkun
Quisling

Surprise
attack on
Denmark
and Norway

33

invasion. It was initially hoped to prevent the Germans from reinforcing and supplying their small invasion force, but the conquest of Denmark had provided the Germans with forward air bases and the limitations of surface navies in an era of military aircraft became clear. The Admiralty did not dare to use its ships in the waters between Denmark and Norway.

The British still hoped to save central and northern Norway from the Germans. Troops landed north and south of Trondheim as a prelude to an advance on the town, but they were not well equipped for fighting in conditions that were still wintry and, above all, the Germans used their complete control of the air to harry them mercilessly. Air power was the key to German success in Norway, in that it overawed the Norwegians at the start and made British operations both by land and sea very difficult later on. After failure round Trondheim, an effort was made to retrieve at least a token prize from a wholly disastrous campaign by the occupation of Narvik. Though the British forces were built up to 20,000 men, the Germans mounted a skilful defence of the town and it did not fall for several weeks. By then, the end of May, a greater disaster was unfolding in France and the British forces were withdrawn from Narvik on 8 June, the day after King Haakon and his government had sailed into exile on a British cruiser.

The Norwegian campaign had been a total fiasco. Whereas the Germans had efficiently co-ordinated their operations by land, sea and air, the British Army and Navy had failed to work well together and little appreciation of the importance of air power had been shown till it was too late. The Germans had achieved great feats by surprise and speed, whereas the British had frequently been cautious and slow and confused about their precise objectives. The result of the botched campaign was a marked deterioration in Britain's strategic position. Germany was able to establish a number of major naval bases on the north-west coast of Europe, which were to prove particularly useful for the U-boats in their campaign to disrupt Britain's supplies from

German air power secures control of Norway

King Haakon of Norway exiled in Britain

America. Sweden, though still nominally neutral, was forced to become a client state of Nazi Germany. Not only did it continue to supply Germany with iron ore, but it allowed German military supplies and troops to cross its territory and built warships for Germany in its shipyards.

Sweden a Nazi client state

Back in Britain the Norwegian debacle inspired a search for someone to blame. The obvious culprit in many ways was Churchill, who had recently been put in charge of a committee to co-ordinate Britain's military effort and had made decisions and interventions which had turned out badly in the course of the campaign. In the end, though, it was Chamberlain who paid the price for the failure of a campaign with which he had little to do. A debate was held in the Commons on the 7 and 8 May 1940. The Labour leader, Clement Attlee made an important point: It is not Norway alone. Norway comes as the culmination of many other discontents. People are saying that those mainly responsible for the conduct of affairs are men who have had an almost uninterrupted career of failure. Norway followed Czechoslovakia and Poland. Everywhere the story is 'Too late'. To switch the focus from narrow issues about the Norwegian campaign to broader ones about the whole course of recent foreign policy was to turn attention from a subject on which Churchill was vulnerable to ones on which his long-held attitudes seemed prescient and relevant. As the politician who had always distrusted Hitler, advocated rearmament and denounced appeasement, he looked to many a more convincing leader of national resistance than Chamberlain, erstwhile champion of appeasement. The result of the debate was not necessarily fatal to Chamberlain, though there were significant Conservative abstentions and votes against the government. There did emerge a clear feeling, though, that Labour should be brought into the government. What was decisive was the decision of the Labour Party executive, meeting at Bournemouth before the party conference, to refuse to allow its leaders Attlee and Arthur Greenwood to serve under Chamberlain, but to permit them to join a government led by someone

Chamberlain
resigns May
1940 else. The Prime Minister at once told his Cabinet colleagues that he would tender his resignation to the King. The question of who was to succeed was still an open one: the contenders were Lord Halifax, the Foreign Secretary, and Churchill. The matter was decided by Churchill's indication, under pressure from his supporters, that he would not serve under Halifax, who declined to make a fight of it. Unlike in 1916, those defeated in the leadership struggle did not refuse to serve in the new government. The War Cabinet of five

War Cabinet
under
Churchill included, besides Churchill himself, Chamberlain, Halifax, Attlee and Greenwood.

When the Commons first met after the reconstruction of the government, Churchill was cheered only by the Labour members. Nevertheless, Churchill was moved to a flight of oratory that events were soon to make even more pertinent than it was when he delivered it:

> I have nothing to offer but blood, toil, tears and sweat... You ask, What is our policy? I will say: It is to wage war, by sea, land and air, with all our might and with all the strength that God can give us ... You ask, what is our aim? I can answer in one word: Victory – victory at all costs, victory in spite of all terror, victory, however long and hard the road may be.

When he uttered these words, Churchill cannot have known just how difficult the road to victory would be. The shattering blow which the Germans were already in the process of delivering would soon make the difficulties much clearer.

3. The Defeat of France and the 'Miracle' of Dunkirk

Germans
invade
Netherlands
May 1940 The Germans invaded the Netherlands on 10 May 1940, some by parachute, most by crossing the land border. The Dutch Army consisted of only eight divisions and retreated in the face of

overwhelming force. The bombing of Rotterdam and the deaths of several hundred civilians persuaded the Dutch to avoid further carnage by surrendering, though Queen Wilhelmina and her government escaped to London. Simultaneously with the attack on the Netherlands came an assault on Belgium. Paratroopers and special forces borne in on gliders seized key bridges and secured the routes into the country, enabling the German advance to proceed with lightning speed. The Belgians had twenty-two divisions and held out for longer than the Dutch, but they did not liaise with the Franco-British forces which came north to meet them, in accordance with the French Plan D. On 28 May the Belgians too surrendered, influenced in their decision by events further south, which made it appear useless to resist further.

Further south the French and British forces were already in a state of collapse. Their defeat was certainly not due to inferiority in numbers of troops or quality and quantity of arms. In no respect were the Allies outclassed and some of their equipment, like the French tank Char B, was superior to anything the Germans had. It was what each side did with its resources that determined the outcome. The Allies had continued to assume that the Germans had not changed their original plan and the dramatic events in Belgium and the Netherlands appeared to confirm their assumption. Their disposition of forces gave the Germans massive local superiority on the Ardennes front. Their 45 divisions had ranged against them only 19 second-rate French divisions. Even this was not enough to guarantee success in a difficult operation like crossing the Meuse, but the commanding general, Kleist, was able to summon a thousand aircraft to his aid to bombard the French positions for eight hours. The French showed no such ability to co-ordinate the different arms of warfare.

It is not wholly surprising that the French failed to take into account a possible attack through the Ardennes. The Germans took extraordinary risks. There were only four narrow and twisting roads through the Ardennes. Along them had to pass according to a tight timetable 134,000 soldiers, 1,200 tanks and 40,000 lorries. There developed what have been called the largest traffic jams yet known in Europe, four 400-kilometre queues. Had the French gained any inkling of what the Germans were doing, their bombers could have wreaked havoc on these slow-moving columns and blocked the roads. Everything depended on the columns keeping going, since if the Germans had failed to achieve speed and surprise, the Allies would have redeployed and the chance of a breakthrough would have been lost. Hence tank drivers and their crews were kept dosed on amphetamines so that they could stay awake for three days and nights. Fuel dumps were established at pre-arranged points, so that vehicles could keep going. Traffic managers in light aircraft and on motorbikes sorted out problems on the roads. The meticulous German planning compels admiration, but it is also evident that an operation so precisely calculated depended on nothing serious going wrong.

Risks of German strategy

The Germans took chances in another way too. They threw all their resources into the business of achieving a decisive result: there were no reserve tank units to help retrieve the situation if (say) the enemy mounted a counter-offensive. The French and still more the British kept much of their air force back, since they were planning for a protracted struggle. As a result, the Germans were often able to achieve local superiority while lacking superiority overall. They were much more profligate with their resources. By the end of May the Luftwaffe had lost nearly a third of the aircraft it started with and many more had been seriously damaged. What mattered to the commanders was battlefield success rather than conserving equipment.

Germans cross the Meuse

The French generals seem to have been quite unable to adjust to the pace of events and the way in which the advent of efficient tanks and aircraft had transformed warfare. Even once the Germans had crossed the Meuse near Sedan, the French commanders failed at once to realise what the German plan was. The Panzer units attacked westwards and crossed northern France very rapidly, helped by the terrain and the dense network of excellent roads and ample local food

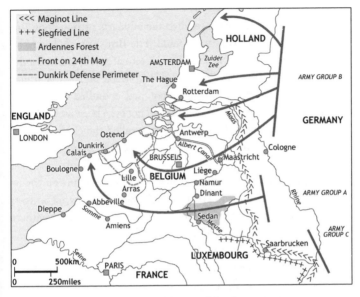

THE INVASION OF FRANCE, MAY-JUNE 1940

supplies. They did not have to reckon with any co-ordinated Franco-British response. Most of the forces which the French might have used to stop the Germans were far off in Belgium. When French tanks tried to intervene, they were usually outnumbered and often out of petrol. Allied aircraft were slow to arrive, often unable to pinpoint their targets and vulnerable to German anti-aircraft fire. As early as 15 May, the French Prime Minister Paul Reynaud telephoned Churchill, 'We have been defeated.' Reynaud dismissed Gamelin, his Commander-in-Chief, but it was too late to retrieve the situation. On 20 May the German forces reached the Channel, so surrounding the Allied forces on three sides, with the sea the only remaining way out of the pocket in which the French and British were now enclosed. Relations between the British and the French broke down, as the British complained of French incompetence and the French of British unreliability.

Germans encircle Allied forces on three sides

Germans
reach
Calais and
Boulogne

By 22 May the Germans reached the outskirts of Boulogne and Calais, cutting the British supply route. The British Army had to be put on half-rations, as it was ordered to retreat to Dunkirk. To the men involved the turn of events seemed inexplicable and demoralising:

Allied retreat
to Dunkirk

much of the equipment which they had trundled round the countryside and were now to abandon had not even been used. Private Alfred Dance of the Rifle Brigade later recalled the confusion and strangeness of the retreat.

> I went on for a day, hiding whenever I saw Germans on the road, until I came across a party of eight British troops, all odds and ends who'd lost their units. There was a corporal with them, but he said we couldn't go any further and we should give up. 'I'm not giving up!' I said… 'My sweetheart's back in England!' We carried on. There was a forest ahead… In the forest we came across a muddy trail. On a nearby tree was a daub of red paint. This paint ran right the way through the forest. It was a guide mark for the troops who had already been through. It took us a day to get through the forest, but when we came out, we could see the British troops heading on the road to Dunkirk. We'd gone right through the Germans.*

To the British High Command, the army seemed doomed as it began to pour into Dunkirk. The town and docks were already under attack from the air. Soon the burning oil depot was filling the air with thick, black smoke. By 26 May the port was wrecked beyond use and the men were ordered on to the beaches. The head of the Luftwaffe, Hermann Goering, had no doubt that his forces could prevent the escape of the trapped men. 'I hope the Tommies are good swimmers,' he said on 26 May. Goering's over-confidence, combined with

---

* Private Albert Dance, quoted in Joshua Levine *Forgotten Voices of the Blitz and the Battle for Britain* Ebury Press, 2006 p.11.

General Rundstedt's desire to conserve his tanks and their crews for the coming operations south of the Loire had influenced Hitler's decision of 24 May to halt the German advance 15 miles from Dunkirk. For some days before Hitler's decision the British authorities had been gathering every available ship – destroyers, transports, ferries, pleasure boats – to form an armada of 850 vessels, that would attempt the rescue of the British Army and as many Allied troops as possible from the Dunkirk beaches. At last on 26 May the evacuation began. It was a laborious process: men had to get into dinghies on the beaches and were then conveyed to the waiting boats. Later the process was speeded up, as a breakwater was used as an improvised jetty and sunken lorries were utilized as a pier. Overcast weather and the pall of smoke gave protection against the Luftwaffe through the last days of May, during which three quarters of the BEF was evacuated. On 1 June the Luftwaffe weighed in, and dive-bombers attacked the beaches and shipping, while circling Messerschmitt fighters offered them protection from the RAF. The RAF flew close on 3,000 sorties, but its aircraft were usually outnumbered. They could not fight over Dunkirk for long because most of their petrol was consumed on the long journeys over the Channel. Still, the evacuation continued, despite a new order from Hitler that the advance by ground forces on Dunkirk should be resumed. By the time Churchill addressed Parliament on 4 June, 338,000 Allied troops had been rescued. The German general Bock visited the scene at Dunkirk as the fighting there drew to an end.

Evacuation
of Dunkirk

The English line of retreat presents an indescribable appearance. Quantities of vehicles, artillery pieces, armoured cars and military equipment beyond estimation are piled up and driven into each other in the smallest possible space. The English have tried to burn everything, but in their haste have only succeeded here and there. Here lies the materiel of a whole army, so incredibly well equipped that we poor devils can only look on with envy and amazement.

Bock's observations make it evident that the Franco-British defeat was not brought about by superior German equipment. Rather, inspired German strategy designed to achieve surprise and apply over-whelming force at the key point, together with meticulous planning, had made the most of equipment that was no more than adequate to inflict on Germany's enemies a catastrophic defeat which put Hitler in control of Western Europe. No doubt, the defeat was primarily a defeat of France, which had provided nine tenths of the joint army, but the BEF had hardly distinguished itself. Most of it escaped from Dunkirk, but it had achieved nothing and had left behind 30,000 men, including 5,000 killed, and all its equipment. Perhaps even more extraordinary than the evacuation which rescued so many men from the debacle was the way in which through the saga of the rescue defeat was converted into a kind of victory. 'Bloody marvellous' was the headline in the *Mirror*. The novelist JB Priestley spoke in a BBC broadcast about how 'the little holiday steamers made an excursion to hell and came back glorious'. Priestley's point was that Dunkirk was the achievement not just of the Royal Navy or of the RAF, but also of ordinary people who supplied and sailed the 'little holiday steamers'.

Dunkirk an achievement of ordinary people

Military defeat was supposed to have produced a mood of national solidarity and defiance which had cheated Hitler at Dunkirk and would in the long run procure his downfall. In the Commons Churchill's flight of oratory as he reported what had happened at Dunkirk sounded a similar note.

Churchill's oratory

Even though large tracts of Europe and many old and famous States have fallen or may fall into the grip of the Gestapo and all the odious apparatus of Nazi rule, we shall not flag or fail...we shall defend our island whatever the cost may be. We shall fight on the beaches, we shall fight on the landing grounds, we shall fight in the fields and in the streets, we shall fight in the hills; we shall never surrender.

In such speeches Churchill was in effect addressing at least three audiences. He aimed to rally domestic opinion behind the war and to build confidence that it could be won. He also implicitly appealed to the Americans for help against the Nazi juggernaut. The daring rescue at Dunkirk had been noticed there. 'As long as the English tongue survives, the word Dunkirk will be spoken with reverence,' predicted the *New York Times* on 1 June. That the 'English-speaking peoples' should stand together was a favourite Churchillian theme. Finally, the Prime Minister's message was one of defiance towards Hitler.

4. Britain Alone against Hitler

It was initially not certain that Britain would decide to defy Hitler. In the dark days of late May, when it was judged unlikely that more than a handful of troops could be rescued from northern France, Reynaud, Prime Minister of France, suggested an approach to Mussolini, who would be invited to broker a European settlement. The Foreign Secretary, Halifax, was in favour of trying out this idea and Chamberlain gave him limited support. Attlee, Greenwood and Churchill were against. Nothing could be worse, Churchill thought, than negotiating from a position of extreme weakness. Even if Britain fought on and was beaten, it would hardly be worse off. Moreover, he was unwilling to subvert the whole rationale of his government, which was that Hitler must be opposed to the bitter end, because no compromise with him that would preserve Britain's essential interests was possible. At a critical point in the discussions in the War Cabinet, Churchill sought an adjournment, during which he addressed the ministers who were not members of the Cabinet. The Labour minister Hugh Dalton recorded that Churchill was 'magnificent', 'the man, and the only man we have, for this hour'. He stressed that he sought to avoid Britain's becoming 'a slave state', with a government 'which would be Hitler's puppet'. The ministers

Settlement with Germany considered

gave the Prime Minister emphatic support. As Churchill recalled, 'Quite a number seemed to jump up from the table and come running to my chair, shouting and patting me on the back.' Until this point, Churchill's position in office had been weak, especially with the Conservative majority. From this point, it became very much stronger and was further enhanced by rhetorical performances which seemed to capture the national mood. Radio gave the Prime Minister access to the people and he used it to secure a massive level of popular support, which an early opinion poll put at 88 per cent in July 1940. He seemed to be adored for his very weaknesses, for plump cigars and excessive quantities of brandy, something which the German propagandists, endlessly harping on them, never understood.

Churchill consolidates his leadership

Churchill's standing among his countrymen might be high, but his standing among the French was very low. The men of the BEF had been saved at Dunkirk, but the 40,000 soldiers of the French rearguard had been left behind. Churchill was condemned for his resolute refusal to send more soldiers or aircraft to assist the French forces still fighting in southern France. He had, surely correctly by early June, already written off the chances of the French recovering from the disasters of May 1940. On 6 June the German armies crossed the Somme on their way south against the remaining French forces. On 12 June Weygand, the Commander-in-Chief, told the French ministers that further resistance was pointless. He predicted that the British would be unable to prevent a German invasion of their island, which meant that France's one option was to seek peace with the new master of Western Europe. He feared too that a revolution might break out in the wake of defeat, as had occurred in 1870, and thought that a rapid peace was the best way to forestall this eventuality. The 84-year old Marshal Pétain, hero of Verdun, became Prime Minister at Bordeaux and on 17 June announced on the radio that it was time to sue for peace. Much of the French Army gave up fighting at this point. A peace agreement was finally signed in the very railway carriage – brought out specially from a museum and put

Pétain becomes Prime Minister at Bordeaux

back in the forest of Compiègne – where Foch and the Germans had signed the Armistice of 1918. France was divided into an occupied zone in the north and along the west coast and a nominally independent state in the south-east, with its capital in the spa town of Vichy and Marshal Pétain as its head of state.

France divided into occupied and Vichy France

'The disgrace is now extinguished. It's a feeling of being born again,' wrote Hitler's propaganda minister Goebbels after Hitler described to him the events in the famous railway carriage. Hitler himself was elated by his astonishing triumph and his popularity in Germany reached its highest point. The SS Security Service reported: 'Admiration for the achievements of the German troops is boundless and is now felt even by people who retained a certain distance and scepticism at the beginning of the campaign.' One reason why the Germans were so delighted was their confident expectation that Britain would now sue for peace and that the war would soon end.

Hitler's popularity in Germany at highest point

Britain's nightmare had come true. The continent of Europe was dominated by a single power, which looked even more overwhelming than Napoleon had after 1807. France and the Benelux countries, which Hitler had just overrun, manufactured sophisticated products such as motor vehicles, aircraft, an array of weaponry and electronic goods. Added to Greater Germany and allied Italy, they formed a bloc of 290 million people whose yearly production exceeded that of the USA or the British Empire. Potentially, the bloc was more impressive still, since the French, Belgians, Dutch and Italians all had large colonial empires. Moreover, the remaining independent countries of Europe hastened to align themselves with ascendant Germany. The overrunning of Norway forced Sweden into virtual satellite status. The news from France led Romania to grant Germany a monopoly of its oil supplies. General Franco in Spain shifted his position from strict neutrality to non-combatant friendship with Germany. Switzerland granted generous export credits to Germany, while restricting exports to Britain. Beyond the circle of minor powers, Italy had already changed its stance. Whereas in September 1939, Mussolini had

Remaining independent countries align with Germany

Mussolini declares war on France and Britain

declined to support Hitler in arms, because his armed forces were unready, by June 1940 he was so anxious to take advantage of the overthrow of the balance of power in Europe that he declared war on France and Britain. He was too late to make a useful contribution to Hitler's overthrow of France and all Italy gained was a demilitarized zone on the French side of the common frontier. Yet Mussolini was now committed to challenging Britain's control of the Mediterranean, forcing Britain to fight there. Hitler's astonishing success was also liable to have an effect on Japan: now that it looked likely that the Far Eastern empires of Britain, France and the Netherlands would be defenceless, Japan might be tempted to turn its attention southwards.

Stafford Cripps fails to break Soviet neutrality

What the USSR would do was anyone's guess, but the new British ambassador to Moscow, Stafford Cripps, had no success in weaning Stalin from his pact with Nazi Germany.

Nonetheless, Britain's position was not as bad as it at first sight looked. Britain was not really alone. Its Empire had rallied to its side. Even more important was the prospective aid of the USA. The giant of the New World was not yet in the war, but from the summer of 1940 it was beginning to turn itself into the world's greatest military power. A peacetime draft aimed to produce a trained force of 2.4 million men. A Two Oceans Navy Expansion Act laid the foundation for vast fleets centred on aircraft carriers. An aircraft production target of 50,000 per annum was set. All this could be done without the Americans having to endure any of the restrictions on consumption that were essential in Germany: civilian consumption was increasing hugely at the time. Britain could not yet draw freely on the products of American industry, since Roosevelt faced an election in November 1940 and dared not too blatantly flout isolationist sentiment. Nonetheless, Britain's continued refusal to come to terms with Hitler, who made an offer, in very imprecise terms, in a speech to the Reichstag (Parliament) on 19 July, was not entirely irrational. The situation was not hopeless.

III

Survival: The Battle of Britain

1. Hitler's Plans

HITLER appears to have expected that after the collapse of their continental ally France the British would make peace with him. His Propaganda Minister Josef Goebbels told his staff in late June, 'A compromise government will be formed. We are very close to the end of the war.' If Britain had made peace, then Hitler could have reverted to the plan sketched out in *Mein Kampf* and got on with securing his hegemony over Europe, free of anxiety about attacks from the west. Hitler admired the British Empire and was quite happy for Britain to keep it, probably because he did not wish to see it dismembered by the Americans, Japanese or Soviets. In his view, then, an Anglo-German bargain was entirely feasible and it was puzzling that the British government could not see that agreement with Germany was the best way of preserving the Empire. He believed that the malign influence of the warmongering Churchill was part of the explanation. Behind him loomed the sinister figure of President Roosevelt, identified by Hitler as the leader of an international Jewish conspiracy against the German race.

Hitler's admiration for British Empire

Interpreting Hitler's thoughts, the German Chief of Staff Halder wrote, 'Invasion is to be undertaken, only if no other way is left to bring terms to Britain.' The British showed no interest in Hitler's hints that he was ready to make peace with them. Inevitably, then, Hitler began to listen to those who had other ideas. One of them was the Foreign Minister Ribbentrop, who had loathed the British ever since his ill-starred stint as ambassador, when he had come to be known as 'Herr Brickendrop'. Ribbentrop advocated invasion and planned to set up a puppet government under Edward VIII, who had been forced to abdicate in favour of his brother in 1936. Schemes were afoot to kidnap

Ribbentrop's plans for puppet government under Edward VIII

Edward, known after his abdication as the Duke of Windsor, and his wife in Portugal, where they were living, but before the scheme could be implemented, Edward accepted the post of Governor-General of the Bahamas, which put him well out of harm's way.

Hitler's consultations about the practicalities of an invasion revealed a depressing picture. The German fleet had been largely destroyed in the Norwegian campaign. Admiral Raeder was reduced to three cruisers and four destroyers, which would have to contest control of the Channel with forty-six capital ships of the Royal Navy's home fleet. It was clear that the British fleet could be neutralized only if the Luftwaffe won total control of the air. Then perhaps the two thousand flat-bottomed river barges that had been assembled in the ports facing Britain could ferry the army across the Channel in what was called Operation Operation Sealion, though they would have required the sea to be like Sealion a mill pond. The enterprise did not seem hopeless: Norway had been conquered in a sea-borne invasion. The head of the Luftwaffe, Hermann Goering, a ruthless and ambitious Nazi politician, gave optimistic assessments of the potential of his forces. He was anxious to enhance his status within the regime by delivering a victory to the Führer. On 1 August Hitler signed the order to launch air strikes Hitler orders against Britain, though by then sporadic air raids had been taking air strikes place for a month. He was not confident of success. If British air and against naval forces were not sufficiently damaged in the prospective Britain campaign, he planned to postpone Sealion till May 1941. August 1940

2. The Combatants

In the Battle of France, the Luftwaffe had distinguished itself; the RAF had not. The German manual for the conduct of air warfare envisaged that land and air forces would co-operate with each other against enemy land and air forces, with the aim of achieving a swift battle of annihilation. This formula had worked extremely well against both the Poles in September 1939 and the French and British forces in May 1940. The RAF did very little to impede the attacks of the Germans in France. The communications system, which involved routing orders to aircraft in France via Bomber Command near London, was far too slow. Most of the aircraft used were Blenheims, which were totally outclassed in daylight fighting: the more effective aircraft were kept back for the defence of Britain. Above all, the RAF had given no thought to the best ways to support the army. The fleets of German dive-bombers had no British equivalents: very few British pilots had been trained in the techniques involved. As the situation in France worsened, squadrons of Hurricanes were released for service across the Channel, but there they lacked the prepared bases and radar warning that they could rely on at home and losses ran at an alarming rate. Spitfires were first used at Dunkirk, where they operated at the extreme limit of their range and were usually outnumbered. Their losses too were high.

Limitations of RAF in Battle of France

After Dunkirk, the war that had to be fought against Germany was the kind of war for which the RAF had prepared. It had been honed as a defensive shield for the British Isles by a career air officer, Sir Hugh Dowding, whose period of office in charge of Fighter Command was twice extended in 1940. The Germans attacked Britain with bombers and dive-bombers which were protected by accompanying fighters. The Germans sought air superiority, which would enable them to drop bombs at will on strategic targets and soften up Britain for invasion. Air superiority involved shattering Fighter Command, since the fighter aircraft which it controlled were the main threat to the fleets of bombers. Fighter Command's objective was to attack the bombers. If possible, they were to be prevented from dropping their bombs, but at least an high rate of loss was to be imposed upon them, in order to deter future attacks. The main threat to the British fighters was the German fighter escorts. The relative strengths of the rival forces of fighters were therefore crucial.

Sir Hugh Dowding, chief of Fighter Command

The British consistently overestimated German fighter strength. Their estimate of German front-line strength for August 1940 was

British over-
estimate
German
fighter
strength

5,800, nearly double the true figure. The Germans, by contrast, underestimated the number of aircraft at the disposal of Fighter Command at the start of the conflict. Both sides tended to exaggerate the number of aeroplanes their men had shot down, largely because of double counting, which occurred when more than one pilot reckoned he had shot down the same plane. After a few weeks of fighting, the Germans became convinced that Fighter Command was about to collapse. For example, Goering announced on 16 September that Fighter Command was down to 177 aircraft, when its real strength was 656. On the British side, the legend of 'the few' developed, given expression by Churchill in a speech to Parliament on 20 August: 'Never in the field of human conflict was so much owed by so many to so few.' In fact, the two sides were remarkably equal at the start of the battle, though the fighters of Fighter Command were spread across Britain, whereas the Germans could concentrate their forces against the south-east. Despite high losses, Fighter Command kept up its numbers better than the Germans. By 1 October German numbers were temporarily down to 275, not much more than a third of those of their enemy.

The
Harrogate
Programme

The British could establish this superiority only because of the success of their arms drive. The Harrogate Programme published at the start of 1940 aimed to produce about 3,600 planes, but in the end over 4,200 were actually built. Churchill's friend the newspaper proprietor Lord Beaverbrook became Minister of Aircraft Production in May, but the basis for the production drive must have been laid earlier. As a result of the great effort, the British built about twice as many planes as the Germans. Not all of these were available for Fighter Command, since substantial numbers had to be deployed to the Mediterranean. Roughly two thirds of Fighter Command's

Hurricanes
& Spitfires

aircraft were Hurricanes, about one third were Spitfires. Both were among the best fighter aircraft of the time. The Hurricanes were a little slower, but were sturdier and the rate of loss was lower. Perhaps the most serious defect of the Hurricane was the position of its fuel tank close to the pilot: if it ignited, he was bound to suffer serious burns. The armament of both aeroplanes also left much to be desired, in that the shot had difficulty in penetrating the armour installed in German aeroplanes.

The Germans depended chiefly on the Messerschmitt 109, possibly the world's best all-round fighter aircraft. Its technical complexity was in one way a disadvantage, since it made for difficulties in raising production quickly. Its armament fired less rapidly than the British fighter weapons, but the explosive shells were more effective in damaging enemy planes. At high altitudes the performance of the Me 109 was much superior to that of the British fighters, but fortunately for the latter, their prime duty of escorting the German bombers forced the Messerschmitts to fight far below 30,000 feet, where their advantage would have been significant. The German bombers proved highly vulnerable to RAF attack. Most of them were slow and obsolescent, but even the newest, the Junkers 88A-1, though fast, had a small maximum bomb-load and weak defensive armament.

Messer-schmitt 109 fighter

Junkers 88 A-1 bomber

Fighter Command was perhaps more worried about the adequacy of its supply of pilots than it was about the number of its aircraft, but the records show that it always had about 1,400 available, a total rising to 1,500 in late September. The Germans had fewer, 1,100 to 1,200, but they could make do, because their rate of loss was lower. The British did not appreciate how short of pilots the Germans were: intelligence estimated that over 7,000 pilots were in operational units. Frantic efforts were made in Britain to raise the supply of pilots. In particular, much use was made of recruits from Europe and the Empire. There were two all-Polish squadrons as well as a Czech and a Canadian squadron. In fact, Fighter Command was more handicapped by shortages of non-combat personnel than by a shortage of pilots. The air stations lacked sufficient mechanics, maintenance workers and signals personnel.

Polish, Czech and Canadian fighter squadrons

Fighter defence was co-ordinated by a system of command and control the heart of which was at Bentley Priory, Stanmore, to the north

of London. Radar stations round the coast relayed by landline
information about incoming aircraft. Their positions were plotted on
a large map table and once the path of the invaders was established,
the information was sent on to the Group Headquarters and the
individual airfields. There was a Group HQ for each of the four large
areas into which Britain was divided. Theirs was the responsibility for
deciding which of the airfields under their control to activate in
response to a given threat, whilst the commanders of individual
airfields decided which squadrons to use. The information had to be
relayed and the necessary decisions taken within a very few minutes,
since enemy aircraft crossed the Channel in only six minutes. Once
air-borne, pilots remained in communication with ground control
through a radio telephonic system.

The system of fighter defence worked thanks to the early warning
provided by radar stations. It had been discovered in 1935 that aircraft
reflect to the ground short-wave radio pulses, which can be captured
on a cathode-ray tube. Twenty-one radar stations were subsequently
built round the coast: they could detect the height and range of
approaching aircraft up to 200 miles distant. Radar could not then
work inland, so that the radar stations had to be supplemented by the
Observer Corps, staffed by 30,000 volunteers, who tracked the aircraft
once they had crossed the coastline and telephoned their findings to
Group HQ and the airfields. Yet more information was supplied by
the RAF wireless interception stations, which took advantage of the
slack radio discipline observed by German aircrew to put together
accurate reports about forthcoming raids. The greatest asset of the
attacking forces was surprise, but to a large extent Fighter Command
managed to deprive them of it.

Perhaps the greatest limitation of the German fighter force was the
short range of the Me 109. But for the conquests of 1940, it could
barely have reached England at all. By the summer of 1940, however,
the Germans could attack Britain from any point on the coastline of
Europe from Norway to Brittany. Only long-range aircraft could

*Command
and Control
Systems*

*Radar
Stations*

*Observer
Corps and
wireless
incerception
stations*

operate from Norway and sorties from there in August showed that losses from the long journey and British action were unacceptably high. The attacks mostly came therefore from more southerly bases. Air Fleet 2 under Hugo Kesselring controlled most of the fighter squadrons clustered in and near the Pas de Calais, where they were closest to Britain, but would still have difficulty in reaching beyond the three south-eastern counties of Kent, Sussex and Surrey. Further south and west was Air Fleet 3 under Albert Sperrle, with a large complement of bombers and dive-bombers expecting to attack naval and coastal targets. Whereas the British had been preparing for air war for some years, the Germans had to improvise. A network of air bases had to be established in northern France, but some deficiencies could not be overcome. An adequate repair organization could not be set up rapidly enough and damaged aircraft often had to be sent back to Germany. The Germans had no way of tracking where the enemy was and could not control the fighter force once it was air-borne.

German airbases in Northern France

3. The Course of the Battle

The term 'Battle of Britain' was used only in retrospect and does not refer, as does, say, the 'Battle of the Somme', to a military engagement with a definite beginning and fought over a definable geographical area. The label is given to the hostilities in the air between Germany and Britain after the fall of France, which on the German side were an attempt to force Britain to make peace and on the British side were an attempt to resist German pressure. The best remembered aspect of the Battle of Britain is the clash of air forces in the skies above England, but much more besides that went on in the summer of 1940.

Coastal Command was required to mount a patrol to monitor German preparations for invasion. There was fear of a possible surprise attack across the Channel during the night and therefore there was continuous reconnaissance of the ports of Belgium and the Netherlands. These operations were costly in terms of lives and

British Coastal Command

equipment: 158 aircraft were lost in six months. Bomber Command was supposed to hit back at Germany to deter it from further attacks on Britain. It was not effective. Its aircraft rapidly proved far too vulnerable in daylight and attacks had to be switched to night-time. In June and July the Ruhr area and north German coast were bombed in an effort to tie down the Luftwaffe and destroy its economic base.

RAF bomb Ruhr and north German coast

Various directives issued in July commanded attacks on invasion ports and a range of industrial targets, such as aircraft factories, oil storage facilities and communication centres. Apart from lack of aeroplanes and pilots to fly them, Bomber Command totally lacked the technology to identify and hit the targets selected. The results of bombing were so random that the Germans could only assume that the British had nothing more in mind than to terrorize the German population.

Deficiencies of Bomber Command technology

Fortunately for Britain, German technology was no further advanced than British. In June and July the Germans sent over small numbers of bombers and dive-bombers protected by fighters. The attacks were designed to probe the British defences and to begin to wear down Fighter Command. Very little wearing-down was achieved and the attacks, though terrifying, achieved little serious destruction or loss of life. The British could perceive no pattern to them and assumed that the Germans were simply spreading terror. The fighters of both sides modified their tactics as a result of experience in the early days of the Battle. The British copied the German tactics of more flexible flying in place of their earlier tight formations. The German fighters found that they had to become less flexible if they were to give adequate protection to their bombers, even though this made them less effective in combat with the British fighters.

The intensity of the fighting increased in August. Goering designated 13 August as *Adlertag* (Eagle Day), which was supposed to mark the start of four days of intensive attacks designed to destroy Fighter Command. Bad weather interfered with these plans, so that the four days stretched into many more and it was a while before the

Adlertag (Eagle Day)

British realized that a new phase of the Battle had begun. There were 32 attacks on fighter stations between mid-August and early September, nearly all of them in the south-east. Thanks to radar and efficient communications, relatively few aircraft were destroyed on the ground and in September, by which time the British had learnt to disperse and camouflage their planes, such losses were almost eliminated. The Germans were convinced by the end of August that at least eight airfields had been knocked out and that the whole system was at breaking point. They were quite wrong. Only three airfields on the Kent and Sussex coast were ever shut down, and then only briefly. Great and successful efforts were made to make bombed airfields operational again. The communications web was the real secret of Fighter Command's success and it held together remarkably well, with the operations rooms of the airfields out of commission on only three occasions. Radar stations were not much damaged either. The Germans pressed their attacks less persistently than they might have done had they realized the role played by radar in the integrated communications system of Fighter Command. With the withdrawal of the Junkers 87B dive-bomber, which had suffered heavy losses, the Germans in any case lost their most effective weapon against radar stations.

Germans over-estimate RAF losses

Junkers 87B withdrawn

The airmen on both sides felt the strain of fighting day after day. The following passage spoken by New Zealander Alan Deere, who flew with the RAF from Hornchurch airfield in Essex, gives some idea of the demands made on a specific individual on one day of the Battle.

We were told to get to readiness, then we were told to go to standby and then we were told to return to readiness so we got out of our cockpits and started walking back to dispersal when the phone rang and we were told to scramble as quickly as possible. So we had to get back to the aircraft, strap in and we were caught taking off. The Germans were already overhead and dropping their bombs. I was held up by a new pilot who got himself in the take-off lane and didn't know where to go. By the time I'd got him sorted out, I was last off and I caught the bombs. I was blown sky high…I was pretty badly concussed and my Spitfire was blown up and I finished up on the airfield in a heap…I had all the hair grazed off the top of my scalp –that's why I haven't much hair now. A doctor plastered me up, bandaged me and said, 'Forty-eight hours and report back.'*

A full account of the strains on the airmen would have also to include reference to the high tension of aerial combat and the toll on the nerves and emotions taken by the deaths of close colleagues. Especially at first, there was a temptation to keep on using the more experienced pilots, but it came to be realized how vital it was to provide relief. Dowding, the head of Fighter Command, ordered that the men must have a full day's rest each week. In the hardest-pressed 11 Group pilots were sent away to enjoy uninterrupted sleep at night. Airfield squash courts were provided in the belief that exercise would help to relieve stress. String bands visited airfields to provide diversionary entertainment. Despite all these palliatives, Keith Park, commander of 11 Group, feared by September that the efficiency of his squadrons was in decline. The problem for the Germans was at least as bad, compounded perhaps by the lack of any clear sign of success.

Strains on airmen

4. The Blitz

Hitler switches attack to British cities

For three weeks Fighter Command had been the chief object of the Luftwaffe's attention, but on 4 September Hitler announced that the main weight of the attack was about to be switched to British cities. London was picked as a major target. The first mass daylight raid on it

* Alan Deere, quoted in Joshua Levine *Forgotten voices of the Blitz and the Battle for Britain*, Ebury Press, 2006 p.273.

took place on 7 September and from then on the city was attacked day and night. Bomber Command had incensed Hitler by an attack on Berlin in late August and the attacks on London were described as vengeance attacks. Yet the change of target was also due to Hitler's appreciation that the achievements of the Luftwaffe during August had been limited. He told his staff on 20 August: 'The collapse of England in the year 1940 is under present circumstances no longer to be reckoned on.' Nonetheless, German intelligence suggested that Fighter Command was at its last gasp, in which case it would be more profitable to attack other targets and possibly produce the collapse which Hitler was waiting for. The new phase began with heavy night attacks on Bristol, Liverpool, Birmingham and other cities, with the aim of destroying industrial, military and transport targets and so sapping the ability and the will to resist. In the instructions for these attacks and for the slightly later ones on London, it was stressed that targets essential to the war should be attacked. Deliberate raids on civilian housing with the object of creating mass panic were ruled out. British instructions to their bomber crews were almost identical.

There were no smart weapons and bombers usually operated in the dark or poor weather, caught in the beam of searchlights and under attack from fighters and anti-aircraft guns. To suppose that they could hit targets of military value with any degree of precision was therefore the merest wishful thinking. Inevitably, they spread destruction in a wide circle round the intended target and the chief victims of most bombing raids were civilians. For example, on the night of 14-15 November there was a heavy raid lasting over ten hours on Coventry. The target was the town's armaments factories, but the medieval cathedral and the commercial buildings of the city centre, together with the working-class housing, were hit. There were 568 people killed in the bombing.

Cities like Coventry could only be attacked by night, since they were too far from the Germans' fighter bases to be given escorts and daylight raids would have been suicidal without them. Daylight attacks on London did appear to be feasible and a number were attempted

First mass daylight air raid on London, September 1940

Night attacks on main British cities

Deliberate attacks on civilian housing ruled out by both sides

Destruction of Coventry

THE BOMBED-OUT SHELL OF COVENTRY CATHEDRAL, 1940
Courtesy of the Imperial War Museum

from 7 September onwards. The German fighters were closely tied to protection of the bombers, which deprived them of all flexibility of manoeuvre. The bombers attacked in three waves. Park ordered his 11 Group to send up six squadrons to deal with the first wave, while another eight waited for the second wave and yet more were ready for the third wave. Fighters were withdrawn from the coastal airfields, where the warning of an attack was too brief to allow the fighters to achieve sufficient height by the time the Germans arrived, and the inland fields were used instead. Park's arrangements reduced Fighter Command's rate of loss and were increasingly effective in destroying enemy planes. During the week 7-15 September the Germans lost 298 aircraft, including 99 fighters. Fighter Command lost 120. Especially bad from the German point of view was 15 September, later

Success of Keith Park's strategy

celebrated as Battle of Britain Day. A quarter of the original 200 bombers were lost, as well as 26 fighters. Such loss rates were unsustainable and it is not surprising that a raid by 70 bombers on 18 September was the last serious daylight raid.

Battle of Britain Day

The German goal of air superiority seemed as elusive as ever. On 14 September Sealion was postponed again and soon afterwards preparations for it were scaled down. By mid-October Germany was maintaining only the appearance of an invasion threat in order to maintain political and military pressure upon England. The attacks on Britain were not called off, however. Hitler still had hopes that a bombing campaign might destroy the British economy and British morale and force the government to the negotiating table even without invasion. 'The decisive thing is the ceaseless continuation of air attacks,' Hitler said at a meeting on 14 September. From mid-September the attacks were almost all at night. The British night-fighter force was composed of Blenheims and Beaufighters, but at first they lacked aerial radar to enable them to find bombers in the dark, so that contact with the enemy was usually achieved by accident. The main line of defence was the anti-aircraft guns. The noise of their firing was reassuring to the population, who felt that something was being done about the German threat, but they were not always effective, since they too found detection of enemy aircraft difficult. German losses were due as much to poor weather and ice as to British action. By the end of the year, the situation was beginning to change, as Ground Controlled Interception radar came to the aid of the Beaufighter and developments in radar also improved the accuracy of the anti-aircraft guns.

Operation Sealion postponed again

Anti-aircraft guns

In case night bombing was insufficient to destroy British morale, the Germans decided that pressure must be applied by day as well. A small group of fighters became fighter-bombers, armed with a single 250kg bomb, and escorted by 200 or 300 combat fighters. The fighter-bombers would maintain the pressure on the population of London already suffering from nights disturbed by bomber raids.

Germany's war of attrition

Fighter Command would be subjected to a war of attrition designed to prevent its recovery from the collapse which it was assumed to have suffered. These raids were extremely numerous, running at around 250 per month in October and November. They took place at above 20,000 feet, where the Me 109 had a distinct advantage over the British fighters. Once again, Fighter Command adjusted its tactics by instituting patrols of high-flying Spitfires to reconnoitre incoming fighters and summon the squadrons in time to prevent the attackers acquiring an advantage of height. Losses of fighter aircraft continued quite high, but the rate of attrition of men and planes never threatened to give the Germans air superiority.

From the time of the raid on Coventry (14 November), provincial cities and ports became major targets of bombing raids, but the sufferings of Londoners were not yet over. The post-Christmas raid of 29 December was one of the fiercest yet launched against the city,

Air raid of 10 May 1941 devastates London

and the raid of 10 May 1941 is reckoned to have been the most devastating night of all. The full moon allowed the bombers to find their targets more easily and low tide meant that there was less water in the river with which to put out the fires started by incendiary bombs. Nearly 2,500 fires were started by the bombing: the resulting conflagration reminded people of the Great Fire of 1666. Fifteen hundred people were killed; 5,000 homes were destroyed; and the damage to historic buildings was enormous. The House of Commons was gutted and the British Library lost a quarter of a million books. The raid seems to have been designed in part to distract attention from the great stroke which Hitler was planning against the USSR. After 10 May the bulk of his forces were directed eastwards. Britain was by

Threat of bombing raids abates

no means free from the threat of bombing raids, but never again was the full might of the Luftwaffe turned against it. Future raids were frightening and annoying rather than lethal threats.

5. The Significance of the Battle of Britain

In the Battle of Britain the German attempt to destroy Fighter Command and achieve air superiority over Britain failed. By the late autumn of 1940 its organization was still intact and it was able to deploy more aircraft and pilots than ever. The switch in September from attacks on the airfields and installations of Fighter Command to the bombing of British cities killed 40,000 people and did a great deal of damage, but little of this hindered Britain's war effort for long and there was no collapse of civilian morale. The conditions under which the invasion plan known as Operation Sealion could go ahead were thus not met and it had to be indefinitely postponed. In all these ways, the Battle of Britain was a British victory.

Failure of German air raids

Yet Hitler had always had serious doubts about Sealion. He had always appreciated how easily an invasion of Britain could go wrong and how ill-equipped Germany in many ways was for launching it, given the quite overwhelming supremacy of the Royal Navy. The highly professional German military planners were all too aware how little all their previous experience of warfare prepared them for an amphibious attack upon England. Apparently, they attempted to learn from the experience of earlier invaders such as the Roman Emperor Claudius and William the Conqueror, but the conditions of 1940 were hardly similar. Amphibious landings on hostile shores required prolonged and extensive preparations and very favourable conditions, as the Allies realized before they launched their cross-Channel invasion of 1944. The Germans had not made such preparations in 1940. Alfred Jodl, Hitler's Chief of Operations, wrote in August 1940, 'It is imperative that no matter what might happen the operation dare not fail.' The risks and the importance of avoiding failure counted heavily against Sealion, but enough preparations were made to demonstrate that Hitler took it seriously and the failures of the Luftwaffe over the skies of England may well have been decisive in its abandonment.

The abandonment of Sealion and the failures of the Luftwaffe did not, on their own, make Britain safe. Churchill always thought that the blockade attempted by the U-boats operating in the Atlantic was a more potent threat to Britain's survival. After its declaration of war on Britain and France in June 1940, Italy posed a mortal threat, not directly to the independence of Britain, but to the survival of its Empire by threatening British control of the Mediterranean and the Middle East. The Germans could, and to some extent did, back Italy up. As the Battle of Britain petered out in the spring of 1941, Britain still had a great deal of defensive fighting to do against the German enemy.

One of the most important results of the Battle of Britain was the lesson which Hitler drew from it. He concluded that despite the control that he had come to exercise over so much of Europe, he was still not in a position to crush a world power such as Britain. His failure in 1940 was above all due to his inability to out-build the British in fighters, to a deficiency in the number of bombers that he could launch against the island and to gross underspending on the navy. His European conquests provided him with substantial booty and a source of labour on which he drew more and more as the war went on. Yet his conquests lacked supplies of oil, many of them also lacked coal, still the main source of power, and the production of food was increasingly inadequate as the import of fertilizers ceased. The productivity of agriculture and industry throughout Nazi-dominated Europe went into inexorable decline. Hitler interpreted the growing economic difficulties as signs that the German *Lebensraum* or living space was still too small.

He believed that Germany needed to make more conquests and acquire more natural resources. It was essential to do this without delay. It was not Britain that Hitler feared. In December 1940, he addressed the Nazi party bosses thus: 'The war is militarily as good as won...England is isolated. It will bit by bit be driven into the ground.' The victory of Fighter Command might have saved

U-boats blockade Atlantic

Germany's need for further *Lebensraum*

Britain from invasion, but it did very little to weaken Nazi Germany, or to make possible an effective attack upon it. Yet behind Britain stood the awesome power of the United States. Safely re-elected, President Roosevelt put forward the idea of 'lend-lease', enabling Britain to order American goods without cash payment. The idea was embodied in a law in March 1941. The supplies were slow to arrive, but it was already clear that the USA would not allow Britain to fail in the war against Germany and that sooner or later it would become an open belligerent. Germany needed to be ready for that eventuality.

US supplies Britain on the 'lend-lease' scheme

The central ideas of *Mein Kampf* once more seemed relevant. In the book Hitler had argued that Russia and the borderlands subject to it possessed the resources which Germany required. The Pact of 1939 gave Hitler access to some of Russia's raw materials but he needed a much more ample supply. He might hope to gain a greater supply by agreement, but he already knew that Stalin drove a hard bargain. There loomed the danger that Germany might become more and more dependent on the Soviet Union. The last thing that Hitler wanted was to become a mere client of the USSR, as Britain was becoming a client of the USA. The only other way of gaining access to the USSR's raw materials was to fight for it. Whereas in the fight with Britain, it was the navy and the Luftwaffe that counted, in a war against the Soviet Union, it was the army that would be decisive. The rapid collapse of France had given Hitler and his generals unlimited confidence in the power of the Wehrmacht to overcome any enemy. As early as July 1940, Hitler turned his mind towards planning for the conquest of the Soviet Union. In the next few months studies suggested that the plan was feasible and on 18 December Hitler ordered his generals to be ready to crush the USSR in a campaign to be launched in the spring of 1941. The Führer argued that a successful war against the USSR would solve his other problems too. By depriving Britain of its last possible continental ally, the campaign would render Britain's struggle entirely hopeless and probably induce

Hitler plans campaign against USSR

it to make peace. In fact, Britain reposed no hopes in the USSR, until Hitler attacked it and made it available as an ally.

In Britain itself, the conflict fought in the skies from the middle of 1940 was not immediately seen as an epic confrontation. The fighter aces remained unnamed to start with, because the RAF did not want to turn some into celebrities at the expense of the rest. Dowding was too prickly to be a universal favourite and he was rapidly retired, while Park was moved to a training command. Gradually, attitudes changed. The appetite of the BBC and the newspapers for heroes had to be satisfied. In March 1941 the Air Ministry published a 32-page account of the Battle of Britain and the events of the summer began to be seen as an important moment in the nation's history. The British began to realize that the unbroken series of foreign policy and military successes which Hitler had hitherto enjoyed had at last come to an end. No one could yet tell how or when Hitler would fall, but defeatism began to give way to the confident expectation that Britain would be victorious in the end. In November 1940 a Gallup Poll found 80 per cent of respondents confident that Britain would win. The outcome of the Battle of Britain had given the people fresh hope.

Battle of Britain boosts morale

IV

The Home Front

1. Evacuation

During the First World War, German airships (Zeppelins) had made over a hundred air raids on Britain and it was confidently expected that there would be far more bombing in another great war. One of the principal tasks of the government was to prepare for the bombing and its consequences. A major difficulty was that no one knew what they would be.

In place of knowledge, there were plenty of alarmist guesses about the likely effects of bombing. In 1938 it was estimated that the Germans would be likely to drop 100,000 tons of bombs in the first fourteen days of war. (The total for the entire war was about two thirds of that.) A ton of bombs was believed likely to produce around fifty casualties, a third of them fatal. This guess seemed to be confirmed as accurate by the experience of Guernica, bombed in daylight on market day during the Spanish Civil War. A huge demand for hospital beds was forecast and local authorities began to lay in large supplies of coffins, usually made of cardboard, since it was cheaper than wood. The impact of bombing on morale was expected to be devastating. The government would be overwhelmed by a people driven mad with terror and would have to sue for peace at any price. Churchill, speaking in the Commons in 1934, envisaged three or four million Londoners driven out of the city into the surrounding countryside, where they would pose impossible problems of accommodation, sanitation and public order. In view of these fears, it is easy to see why the government drew up plans for an orderly evacuation of areas considered likely targets of enemy bombing, to be implemented well before the attacks began.

Early
evacuation of
school-
children

Plans were made for the evacuation of four million primary schoolchildren with their teachers and mothers with children under five. Unexpectedly, many inner-city people were not willing to part with their children and only about a third of the anticipated number took up the offer of evacuation. Even so, the migration was on an enormous scale. It was set in motion on 1 September 1939, when crocodiles of London children were shepherded by their teachers from school to the local railway station, where one of the four thousand special trains was waiting for them. Others left on special buses and passenger ferries. Difficulties emerged when the children arrived at their destinations. Local billeting officers were responsible for placing the new arrivals, which was usually done by means of a process often described as similar to a slave auction. Inevitably, some children, the uglier, the diseased, those inseparable from a sibling, were hard to place and the officer might have to use his powers of compulsion to foist them on an unwilling host.

The rural hosts usually knew nothing of life in inner-city slums and were often appalled to find that their guests suffered from infestations of head-lice, that they had no idea what pyjamas were, or that they were unfamiliar with flush toilets. Bed-wetting was a frequent reaction to the stress of the evacuation, and it did not endear the guests to their hosts. Evacuees frequently arrived with unsuitable or inadequate and worn-out clothing, but the local authorities were given hardly any money to assist hosts in kitting out the children. Hosts might have to dip into their own funds, though in some cases children were simply left to shiver. Mothers who came with small children often had difficulties in fitting into a household managed by someone else with different customs and values and sorely missed the recreational facilities of their home areas. It was true that rural and urban Britain got to know each other better thanks to the experience of evacuation, but knowledge did not always produce understanding, let alone liking, on either side. Still less did the evacuation do much to bridge the class divide in mid-20th-century Britain. By and large, the government evacuation scheme became a matter of the rural poor housing the urban poor. Billeting officers found it difficult to press wealthier and more powerful people to take evacuees. When they did open up their houses, they were much more likely to accommodate some of the two million who made their own arrangements for evacuation and were usually a 'nicer class of person'.

It was unfortunate that the evacuation had been set in train without any consideration of when the Germans were likely to start bombing raids, which were not practicable till the Germans overran northern France. In the absence of danger, within four months close on 900,000 evacuees had returned home. There was a renewed, but this time unofficial, exodus when the bombing started in earnest, and there were still over a million evacuees late in 1944. Many of the evacuees later went on to give accounts of their experiences, which were, of course, very varied, many life-enhancing, some horrifying. The end of evacuation could be as traumatic as the beginning had been. Some found the transition from the countryside back to the town very difficult. Many returned to bombed-out areas, where the housing stock was inadequate and there was no house for them. Some parents and their children had been so long apart that they could no longer recognize each other. Over 5,000 children failed to find any parents, perhaps because they had perished in the Blitz.

Evacuees return home during Phoney War

2. The Impact of the Blitz

Very large numbers were evacuated, but still more people had simply to put up with the bombing. In British folk memory, the defining experience of the Second World War was enduring the German bombing raids. In this war, more than in any previous one, it was not just the members of the British armed forces who were put to the test, but also the ordinary civilian population. In folk memory at least, they came through the ordeal triumphantly and even discovered a new and greater unity in adversity.

Post-war myth-ologizing of the Blitz

London
Under-
ground air
raid shelters

The theme of unity in adversity is supremely well illustrated in Henry Moore's Shelter Drawings. Moore was primarily a sculptor, but during the war he worked for the War Artists' Commissioners. His famous Shelter Drawings were inspired by nocturnal visits to the London Underground stations, which from September 1940 were used as night shelters from the falling bombs by an estimated 177,000 people. Moore's sleepers are not individualized and there are no details that might suggest their class origins. He stresses what unites them: the gentle, mysterious lighting of these spaces beneath the blacked-out city, the swelling curves of the blankets which link the recumbent figures one to another. Yet Moore's drawings do not tell the whole story. He visited the shelters in the early days. When he became Home Secretary, Herbert Morrison put arrangements on a more organized footing, by installing bunk beds and providing proper sanitation and mobile canteens and issuing tickets for regular users. Inevitably, some people sought individual profit from the common ordeal and a black market in tickets arose: they changed hands for 2s 6d per night. In any case, sheltering in the Underground was not a typical experience. Most Londoners endured the Blitz in their own homes, perhaps seeking refuge in an Anderson shelter in the garden or a Morrison shelter – a reinforced steel table beneath which families could take refuge – within the house. Purpose-built communal shelters were mostly shunned, partly because they were cold, airless and poorly lit, but also because feelings of solidarity did not override people's attachment to their own homes. Besides, staying at home enabled people to defend their property against those who took advantage of the common misfortune to enrich themselves by looting.

The experience of being bombed was terrifying. A stretcher bearer at West Ham said, 'I watched a bomb drop. One house collapsed under it and as it did, three or four houses folded on to it just as though they were a pack of cards.'* He must have been watching a high-

---

* Albert Prior, quoted in Joshua Levine op. cit. p.321.

HENRY MOORE'S STUDY FOR *TUBE SHELTER PERSPECTIVE*, 1940-41
Courtesy of the Henry Moore Foundation

explosive bomb, which came in a number of sizes. In addition, there were incendiaries, which burned fiercely for ten minutes and set fires going; some of them then exploded. Landmines were also dropped: they were adapted shipping mines, which were dropped by parachute and caused enormous damage. Such attacks on civilians were expected

Mass
Observation

to cause a collapse of morale. When this did not happen, the press tended to attribute to the population extraordinary qualities of heroism and resilience in extreme conditions. Mass Observation, a private social research agency, which had been set up in 1937 in order to check and challenge official views of what public opinion was, often presented a different picture. After bombing raids on the East End of London in September 1940, Mass Observation reported:

> The whole story of the last weekend has been one of unplanned hysteria ... Of course the press version of life going on normally in the East End on Monday are grotesque. There was no bread, no electricity, no milk, no gas, no telephones ... The press versions of people's smiling jollity and fun are gross exaggerations. On no previous investigation has so little humour, laughter or whistling been recorded.

Significantly, this report related to an early raid. The initial shock of the bombing was very great, but people could and did get used even to life in the shadow of the bomber. Looking back on his experience, a London milkman said:

> Every night was the same. They came over and every morning you'd go out and find another building gone down or another row of shops destroyed. You got used to it. After about three months, if Jerry didn't come over, you thought he was on holiday. You got a night's sleep.*

Buckingham
Palace hit

Despite the persistent problem of looting, a degree of social solidarity was promoted. All social groups suffered. Even Buckingham Palace was hit several times and the Queen was reported to have said that she was glad of it, because it enabled her 'to look the East End in the

---

* William Gray, quoted in Joshua Levine op.cit. p.320

THE HOME FRONT

ST PAUL'S CATHEDRAL IN THE BLITZ, 29 DECEMBER 1940
Courtesy of the *Daily Mail* Archives

eye' on her many tours of bombed-out areas. Those whose houses were not destroyed had often to shelter relatives and neighbours who had not been so fortunate. More and more people too served as fire-watchers, who had to locate fires caused by incendiaries before they took hold, or as auxiliary fire-fighters, or had to help the community to survive the Blitz in some other way. Two hundred people enlisted as volunteers for St Paul's Watch: their job was to help to save Wren's great cathedral during the bombing. Quite apart from its spiritual and

Symbolic importance of St Paul's Cathedral

aesthetic value, it was thought essential to morale to save such an iconic landmark from destruction. One of the most powerful images to emerge from the war was a photograph taken from the roof of the *Daily Mail* offices by Herbert Mason.

Dome of
St Paul's
Cathedral
struck

It was taken during the raid of December 29th, when the cathedral had to be saved from an incendiary bomb that lodged in the dome, and shows the dome and towers bathed in light above clouds of smoke from the burning city. It became a symbol of indomitable British spirit and of its ultimate survival.

John Piper,
Official War
Artist

The photograph presents a striking contrast to the oil painting done by official war artist John Piper, who painted the bombed shell of Coventry Cathedral in November 1940. He depicted windows 'empty, but for oddly poised fragments of tracery, with spikes of blackened glass embedded in them' and 'red-grey façades, stretching eastwards from the dusty but erect tower and spire'. The spire, caught in light, perhaps suggests that this cathedral and perhaps Coventry too will rise again from the ashes. If so, this was not a view that the people of Coventry seem at first to have shared. Mass Observation reported as follows: 'People feel the town itself is dead, finished, and the only thing to do is to get out altogether.' Mass Observation was inclined to blame the civic authorities, who had given priority to disposal of the dead and had neglected to attend to survivors' immediate needs, by providing mobile canteens, loudspeaker vans to give people information and social workers to assist the bereaved, homeless and orphaned. What did amaze observers was the speed with which the people of the city recovered after the initial shock. A Coventry civilian later said: 'I would rate Coventry folk as being a shining example to the nation during the war. People who'd lost their homes continued turning up for work in the factories.'* They did so even at the Morris engine works, which had lost its roof. No doubt, the best way of

---

* Thomas Cunningham-Boothe, quoted in Levine op. cit. p.393.

recovering from the ordeal was to hold on to as many of the routines of ordinary life as possible.

Probably, the most important factor in the ability of communities to cope with bombing raids was the competence of their local authorities. The council in Coventry had been taken by surprise. Others were better prepared and organized. In Hull, for example, 40,000 people were billeted within two days of a major raid and 110,000 emergency repairs to houses were carried out. In Sheffield huge numbers of emergency meals were provided within 24 hours of a raid and within four days everyone had been re-housed. In Liverpool, by contrast, Mass Observation reported 'unprintably violent comments on local leadership' from all sections of the community. Elements of the population looked for someone to blame and there was an outbreak of xenophobic attacks against Jews, Greeks and the Chinese.

Outbreaks of xenophobia

The 'Blitz spirit' has often been too much idealised. Yet pre-war fears and German hopes of a collapse of British morale under the impact of enemy bombing were never realised. In some places community cohesion was threatened, but it was usually short-lived and overall, communities were, indeed, strengthened. Hatred of Germans never reached the heights of hysteria that it attained in the First World War, but almost everyone accepted that the Germans had to be beaten. Perhaps the attitudes reported by Oliver Bernard, a child in London at the time, were typical.

You used to hear, 'Bloody Jerry!' or 'Old Adolf's having another go at us!' but it was half-jokingly said and felt ...Very few people realised how incredibly horrible the Nazis were. I already knew that from my Jewish friends but it hadn't got to most people what their true character was. They were just our adversaries.[7]

---

* Oliver Bernard, quoted in Levine op.cit.p. 414.

3. The War and Class Antagonism

The lesson had been learnt in the First World War that war led to shortages of food and consequently to high prices which put staple foods beyond the limited means of the poor. In order to avoid social division and unrest, it was necessary for the government to intervene with a policy of rationing, which was duly introduced in January 1940, despite a vigorous press campaign against it. Everyone had to register with and buy their food from chosen shops. Everyone was issued with ration books and as they bought the weekly ration of the foods included in the system, the shopkeepers crossed off the relevant items in the books. At first, only bacon, butter and sugar were rationed, but gradually the system was extended to include most foods consumed on a mass scale. Naturally, items had to be consumed in a standard form; there was little room for choice. Prices were controlled by the government, which brought in food subsidies as early as November 1939. From an initial £72 million per annum the cost climbed to £250 million in 1945. Vulnerable groups, such as nursing mothers and young children, were given certain basic foods free. The government varied the amount of different foods which people could buy in accordance with the expected supply. People were encouraged to supplement the rations fixed by the government through 'digging for victory', which meant turning gardens into vegetable patches or cultivating allotments, which in many cases were created by digging up public parks and other open spaces.

Rationing introduced Jan. 1940

In view of the German U-boat threat to British food supplies, there was no alternative to the government's policy, and the government's boast that the very poor ate better during the war than they had ever eaten before was probably true. Nonetheless, the government was not able to still all criticism. The government's research agency Home Intelligence reported in the middle years of the war: 'People are inclined to blame vitamin deficiency in the wartime diet for the prevalence of skin troubles, indigestion, colds and general debility, and to feel some resentment of official statements that "The health of the nation is better than before the war".' In fact, the problem was probably the shortage of food and the lack of variety rather than lack of essential nutrients and there was little the government could do about either. There were complaints too that the privations of war did not bear equally on everyone. Items categorized as luxury foods were not rationed and if people could pay the high prices which grapes, or melons, or bottles of wine commanded, then they were able to enjoy a much more varied diet than those who had to subsist on their rations. Lord Woolton, the Minister of Food, also received many complaints because the rich could evade the privations imposed by rationing by eating out in restaurants. The government decided that extending the rationing system to include restaurant meals was administratively unfeasible, but a chain of government-run and modestly priced eating establishments called British Restaurants was set up to enable the working classes to supplement their rations with the occasional restaurant meal.

Lord Woolton, Minister of Food

From June 1941 clothes too were rationed, so that British textile factories could turn as far as possible to the manufacture of uniforms and parachutes rather than civilian clothing. Each item of clothing was given a value in coupons and each individual was allowed sixty points in coupons per year. Clothes prices were not regulated and the wealthy were in effect able to make their points go further by purchasing clothes of better quality that were more durable. Other people might have to follow government advice to 'make do and mend'. In this respect too, then, British citizens were not exactly all equal in adversity, but they were a great deal more equal than they had ever been before.

There was also considerable redistribution of income in the course of the war. Increased rates of tax on higher incomes hit the middle class, while the working class was assisted by price controls and food subsidies as well as by higher wages. The purchasing power of the poorer sections of the community seems to have increased by about a

Re-distribution of income

quarter during the war years. In part, this change was due to the scarcity of labour during the war, but it was also the result of a government that was sympathetic to the working class. When Churchill formed his government in May 1940, Ernest Bevin, General Secretary of the Transport and General Workers Union, became Minister of Labour and National Service. His appointment signified the appreciation by the government of the paramount need to achieve the co-operation of the trade unions in the war effort. As early as 25 May 1940, Bevin appealed to the TUC for its support and in its General Secretary Walter Citrine he found an eager partner. A Joint Consultative Council, composed of seven representatives of the employers and seven trade unionists, was established to advise on economic planning. The trade unions were installed at the heart of government to an extent that had never been the case between 1914 and 1918. The government's propaganda emphasis on fighting a 'People's War' further enhanced the position of the unions. The newspapers, newsreels and feature films stressed the 'battle for production', implying that its importance was as great as that of the military campaigns. If that were so, then the trade unions were as significant as the army officers.

The powers vested in Bevin as Minister of Labour were enormous. He was empowered to direct 'any person in the United Kingdom to perform any service required in any place'. Perhaps only the USSR had a more comprehensive system of labour direction. Workers could be compelled to stay in jobs – in munitions, mining and agriculture, for example – defined as essential. Under Order 1305 strikes and lockouts were banned and compulsory arbitration of disputes could be ordered. Bevin realized that though Order 1305 might have a useful deterrent effect, it would in practice be hard to enforce. In keeping the workers onside, the government and the employers were inclined to rely more on concessions, especially higher wages, than on their draconian powers. Even so, industrial peace was not unbroken. One

Trade unions and the War effort

Strikes and lockouts banned

of the most serious disputes was that at Betteshanger colliery in the Kent coalfield in 1942. The bone of contention was the perennial issue of allowances for working difficult seams. When a strike was declared, the government prosecuted those involved: three local trade union officials were sent to prison and over a thousand miners were fined. Uproar in the labour movement and sympathy strikes elsewhere led to Herbert Morrison, the Home Secretary, releasing the prisoners and most of the fines were never paid. The Betteshanger dispute shows that longstanding, deeply felt grievances were not forgotten because of patriotic enthusiasm. Old animosities lived on too. Mass Observation studied the northern industries in 1942. Their reporter concluded: 'One looked in vain for any sign of a unity binding all parties in the fight against Germany. From the men, one got the fight against the management. From the management, one experienced hours of vituperation against the men.' In 1943 no fewer than 3.7 million days work were lost to strikes. Against this background, the government introduced Defence Regulation 1AA, which laid down maximum penalties of a five-year jail sentence and a £500 fine for incitement to strike. The government never actually made use of the Regulation, but its very adoption reveals some of the fears and tensions which lay behind the façade of national unity.

Yet when the complaints about the well-to-do enjoying preferential treatment, the conflicts between employers and their workers and the difficulties of the government in preserving industrial harmony have all been listed, the fact remains that a long and difficult struggle against Nazi Germany and its allies revealed surprisingly few dangerous fault-lines in British society. No one and nowhere played the role that Red Clydeside or South Wales played in the First World War. As George Orwell remarked, the British fought the war as a family, though, like all families, they experienced moments of discord.

4. Women and the War

The Second World War, like the First, was a total war in which it was unthinkable to exempt half of the population from contributing to the war effort. When Ernest Bevin acquired powers to conscript labour, therefore, they were understood to include the power to mobilize the female half of the population. In 1941 women between the ages of twenty and thirty were conscripted for war-work or for service in the women's branches of the armed forces. Later, the upper age limit was extended to fifty.

Far more women joined the armed forces than had done so in any previous war, though their roles and their pay were limited. For Women's Royal Navy Service (Wrens) example, 75,000 Wrens (so called from the initials of the Women's Royal Navy Service) were employed as drivers and clerical and domestic staff in order 'to free a man for the fleet'. In time, shortages of male personnel led to women manning anti-aircraft guns at naval bases, working on decrypting enemy naval communications and acting as dispatch riders. There were twice as many Waafs (in the Women's Auxiliary Air Force). Like the Wrens, they did not fight. To start with, they were usually plotters, whose job was to plot the path of incoming enemy aircraft on the map tables in the operations rooms attached to airfields. As time went on, they came to serve as engineers and mechanics, to refuel aircraft and to operate barrage balloons. This extension of their duties reflected in part a shortage of men, but also the growing realization that women were capable of performing this wider range of roles perfectly competently. The Army equivalent of the Wrens and the Waafs was the ATS or Auxiliary Territorial Service. Whereas the Wrens and the Waafs relied on volunteers, most of them middle class, most members of the ATS were working-class conscripts, so that this was viewed as the Cinderella service, an opinion that was encouraged by the inelegant khaki uniforms which the girls had to wear. The members of the ATS were employed as clerks, drivers and cooks.

Women's Royal Navy Service (Wrens)

Women's Auxiliary Airforce (Waafs)

Auxiliary Territorial Service (ATS)

If men did not at first believe that women could be competent in tasks that had no connection with traditional female roles, equally many people were inclined to suppose that, once removed from the protection of their families, women were likely to engage in immoral practices. Essentially, this was the view that the only proper place for a woman was in the home in another guise. The persistent rumours prompted the government to set up a parliamentary committee to investigate. It conclusively proved that there was almost no substance in the gossip about female members of the armed forces.

Substantial numbers of women were also enlisted as Land Girls in the Land Army. Agriculture was still a labour-intensive industry and it became chronically short of labour after large numbers of workers joined the armed forces or went into war industries, where they were paid much better than farmhands were. Bevin helped to slow the drift from agriculture by enforcing improved minimum wage rates in the industry, but the Land Girls were a useful additional source of labour on the farms. Their numbers were much increased as the U-boat threat made it essential to maximise domestic production of food: by 1944 there were 80,000 of them. Two thirds of them were country girls by origin, but one third were recruited from urban areas. Memoirs written by the girls later suggest that being a Land Girl was not a soft option. The work was usually physically demanding and had to be carried on in all weathers. Quite often the girls felt isolated and had to put up with accommodation in empty labourers' cottages which might lack all modern facilities, such as gas, electricity and running water. They were at the mercy of the farmers too, who might see them as a convenient source of cheap labour.

Not much more than half a million women were involved in the armed services and the Land Army at any one time. The numbers employed in industry ran into millions. Paving the way for huge numbers of extra women to join the workforce was not easy, but Bevin liaised closely with the trade unions, which agreed to let women in and to allow jobs traditionally done by skilled men to be done instead

Land Girls

Moves towards equal pay

by the semi-skilled, provided that everything reverted to the previous status quo at the end of the war. Women were also to be given the same pay that men had received, though this concession was hedged about by various qualifications. It was still generally assumed that women should be paid less than men, as was shown in 1943, when Rolls Royce brought in untrained male and female workers to operate machines at Hillington near Glasgow and immediately put the men on a higher rate of pay. On this occasion, the discrimination was so blatant that the women went on strike and succeeded in extracting concessions. Significantly, when the women held a demonstration in Glasgow, people did not side with the women, but pelted them with eggs and tomatoes.

Perhaps the relatively poor wages they were offered helped to account for women's initial reluctance to volunteer for war work. Advertising campaigns were run during War Work Week and slogans were used, such as 'Don't queue like shirkers, join the women workers.' This slogan was supremely untactful, in that it implied that women who were not employed in industry were sitting idle at home. Since married women had to run the household, this was far from true of most of them. The government adverts ignored the fact that a married woman at work had a double burden to bear: the paid work and her unpaid tasks as wife and mother. For many, it was hardly possible to accept employment outside the home unless childcare facilities were provided. The Ministry of Labour accepted this necessity and was keen to provide the service, but the Ministry of Health dragged its feet, fearing the breakdown of family life. By the start of 1941, there were only fourteen government-sponsored nurseries. Mothers staged 'baby riots', stopping traffic with their prams and chanting, 'We want war work, we want nurseries.' Their success was only partial: there were never places in nurseries for more than a quarter of working mothers and most had to depend on private arrangements.

'Baby Riots' over childcare for working mothers

As far as women were concerned, the story of the Second World War was remarkably similar to that of the First. Many of the same arguments with male-dominated trade unionists had to be rehearsed. Once again, women appeared to make some advances in the workplace towards equality with men. And once again the vision of equality proved to be a mirage. The modest advances towards equal pay or towards the provision of childcare facilities for working women were largely reversed as soon as the war was over. The government was not prepared to initiate a social revolution in the middle of a great war: it dared not disturb the national consensus at a time when national unity was essential. Hence the issue of equal pay for women was handed over to a Royal Commission, which reported when the war was over. Perhaps the main difference between 1918 and 1945 was that in the former year vocal female pressure groups had decided what they wanted in return for their contribution to the war effort, the vote, whereas in 1945 women had not organized behind any specific demand.

Promise of equality a mirage

5. Government Power and Control

The First World War had brought an enormous increase in the power of government and the control which it exercised over society. The Second World War was no different in this respect. The government spent far more of the national income. In 1939 government expenditure was about £1 billion; by 1945 it was £6 billion, amounting to around two thirds of the national income. The government acquired far more bureaucrats to assist it in regulating society. Before the war began, there had been about 387,000 civil servants; by the time it ended, there were over 700,000.

Expansion of government and the Civil Service

Enforcement of the government's detailed economic regulations required close supervision of society. Lord Woolton, the Minister of Food, had to hope that heavy penalties for selling food otherwise than through the rationing system would act as a sufficient deterrent to selling it on what was called the black market. Yet despite his 900 inspectors, the profiteers' chances of getting caught were never high and the profits they could make were considerable. Large numbers of goods were price-regulated and Regulation Committees were kept busy hearing complaints against shopkeepers who had overcharged by minute sums. Where the public had no interest in bringing charges, however, it was likely that nothing would happen. After France was liberated, large amounts of goods that were scarce in Britain, such as cosmetics, perfumes and silk stockings, were illegally brought in and sold on the black market at inflated prices. The customers were only too happy to get the goods at any price, whilst relevant officials were too swamped by the volume of work and bemused by the complexities of the regulations to intervene successfully.

Black Market profiteering

The government was concerned not only to regulate the economy, but also to control the flow of information. A Ministry of Information was set up with the job of co-ordinating the processing of all government information and propaganda. The rapid turnover of ministers in charge of it is indicative of its lack of success. Its encouragement to people to snoop on their neighbours was not well received, and there was much criticism of police prosecutions for idle talk, for example comments which seemed to indicate approval of Hitler. Its posters and propaganda films seem to have met with bored cynicism. Its censorship of the press was never complete, despite the authoritarian instincts of some ministers, since the government could not afford to seem too much like that of Nazi Germany. Most of the newspapers thought it their duty to toe the government line, but a couple got into trouble with the government. The Communist *Daily Worker* opposed the war while Stalin was allied to Hitler and was duly suppressed. The *Daily Mirror* positioned itself as the mouthpiece of the ordinary citizen or soldier and was critical of the authorities, a stance which was very popular, to judge by its high circulation figures. The government disliked the paper's critical spirit. Churchill wrote to the proprietor, Cecil King, as follows: 'There is a spirit of hatred and malice against the government which surpasses anything I have

Ministry of Information and Propaganda

Censorship

ever seen in English journalism. One would have thought that in these hard times some hatred might be kept for the enemy.' The newspaper was threatened with closure over a cartoon which Churchill misinterpreted, but in the end was let off with a severe warning. It was not only newspapers that were censored. Noel Coward's ironical song 'Don't let's be beastly to the Germans' was banned by the censors, whose lack of a sense of humour could sometimes make them ridiculous.

In the Second World War the radio was a major source of news for most people. During the Phoney War, when the BBC had little news to report, many people seem to have supposed that news was being kept from them and they tuned into various German propagandist radio stations. The *Daily Express* invented the name 'Lord Haw-Haw' for the leading German broadcaster. It was applied to several different men, but chiefly to William Joyce, who was born an American but had emigrated to Britain and become a follower of Sir Oswald Mosley. He went to Germany at the start of the war and became the most effective broadcaster to Britain. To start with, some listeners accepted his view that the war was a product of a Jewish conspiracy, but his British audience listened primarily to pick up news that their own government might have kept from them.

BBC radio broadcasts

The BBC was nominally independent of government, but in practice advisory civil servants had a great deal of control over its output of news and indeed over its output in general. Nonetheless, the BBC came through the war with its reputation enhanced. It enabled the Prime Minister to address British citizens in their own homes: his broadcasts after the 9 pm news were listened to by half the population in 1941. It relaxed the austere standards of Lord Reith by adding to the Home Service the Light (originally the Forces) Programme. One of its notable stars was Vera Lynn, nominated the 'Forces' Sweetheart' in a *Daily Express* poll. She and her quartet performed and broadcast songs requested by the soldiers. The songs with which she was particularly associated were the sentimental favourites 'We'll Meet Again' and 'The White Cliffs of Dover'. One function of the BBC in wartime was to cheer people up, which it did most successfully with a fast-paced comedy programme called ITMA, or *It's That Man Again*.

During the war, the government came to feel that it needed more control over people who might prove dangerous than it usually required in peacetime. Tribunals were at once established to vet 60,000 refugees, mostly from Germany and Austria, and about 13,000 other foreign nationals residing in the country in order to assess the risk they posed to the country's security. At first, it was thought necessary to intern under 600, with a few thousand more subjected to various controls, but Hitler's amazing run of successes in 1940 were put down to the activities of Germans who had earlier entered the countries concerned and there was increasing anxiety about the possible activities of such people in Britain too. Lack of any clear evidence did not prevent the spread of an essentially irrational hysteria, which led eventually to the internment of over 27,000 people. The conditions in which they were kept were often dire, partly because numbers increased so rapidly. It was also considered that the Germans might be assisted by native British sympathisers. Regulation 18B allowed the arrest of British nationals who acted in a manner prejudicial to public safety or the defence of the realm and an amendment to it allowed the Home Secretary to arrest anyone likely to act in this manner. A few dozen people belonging to a variety of right-wing groups, such as the British Union of Fascists, were arrested, including Sir Oswald and Lady Mosley, perhaps more because of public clamour than because the government feared them. The BUF had only 9,000 members in 1939 and other far right groups were smaller still. Mosley even commanded his followers to aid the defence, should there be an invasion. The government was more worried about the Communist Party with 20,000 paid-up members and a newspaper read by 90,000, but there was never any evidence that the party had any influence on popular attitudes to the war and the government did not take action

Internment of enemy nationals

Arrest of Sir Oswald and Lady Mosley

against it, though it considered doing so. After mid-1941 the government and the Soviet-supporting Communists were supposed to be on the same side, though even Labour leaders continued very wary of these new allies.

In many respects, Britain's wartime government between 1939 and 1945 did what previous wartime governments had done. Like the governments of the revolutionary and Napoleonic period and that of the First World War, it rode roughshod over traditional freedoms from arbitrary arrest, of free speech and of the press. It probably had less need to do so, since at least from May 1940 the war seems to have been backed by a national consensus more complete than in any previous war. As always in war, taxation went up to levels that were wholly unprecedented. *Laisser faire* and economic individualism had been in retreat for a century, but the Second World War went even further than the First in the imposition of government control on the economy and society. Usually, at the end of wars, there was an irresistible urge to return to the pre-war situation which was considered as normal and right. The big question on the home front was whether this would happen once again when the Second World War ended.

Consensus supports war

V

THE WAR IN THE MEDITERRANEAN

1. The Mediterranean in 1940

Importance of Mediterranean to British Empire

ALL through the 19th century Britain had regarded control of the Mediterranean as one of its basic interests. The Mediterranean was the highway to the Middle East, through which lay Britain's lines of communication to India. Its possession of Gibraltar, acquired from Spain in 1704, safeguarded British entry to the Mediterranean. The island of Malta had become a British possession during the Napoleonic wars: it controlled the narrow passage between Sicily and Tunisia from the western to the eastern Mediterranean. In the eastern Mediterranean Britain had acquired the island of Cyprus in 1878,

Suez Canal

but the building of the Suez Canal in Egypt had made it imperative for Britain to control that vital link to the Indian Ocean. Accordingly, Egypt had been occupied by Britain in 1882 and ever since the British had exercised indirect control over the country and had stationed troops at the Canal. Further east still, Britain exercised great influence in countries like Iraq, which were becoming important as sources of an increasingly vital commodity, oil.

It was evident to Hitler's advisors, as they considered what to do about Britain in the late summer of 1940, when it became ever less likely that Operation Sealion would go ahead, that one option was to strike at Britain's position in the Mediterranean. This course of action offered important advantages. If successful, it might force Britain to terms and hence safeguard Germany from attack in the west if and when the planned attack on the USSR went ahead. Even if Britain still held out, it might at least be tied down until its last hope, the USSR, had been vanquished. Maybe a Mediterranean strategy would be so successful that it would render an attack on the USSR unnecessary. The German Navy hoped that this might be so, since naval power would play a much larger role in a Mediterranean strategy than it would in an overland onslaught on the USSR. Success in the Mediterranean could solve Germany's central problem of lack of resources, by opening up the oilfields of the Middle East and the resources of Africa.

Another attraction of a Mediterranean strategy was that Germany might be able to get others to do much of the fighting. Accordingly, in the autumn of 1940, Hitler sounded out his allies concerning their willingness to co-operate in a Mediterranean strategy against Britain. He had hopes for a joint attack on Gibraltar with Franco, the Spanish dictator. The fact was, however, that Franco had only recently won a hard-fought civil war. He could not contemplate involving his country in war without a great deal of help from Germany. The deliveries of foodstuffs and arms that he required were far beyond what Germany could afford to supply. Only an appeal to Franco's considerable greed for territorial gains might have induced the dictator to commit himself, but Hitler had nothing to offer beyond Gibraltar. The gains in Morocco which Franco asked for would have been at the expense of France, but Hitler was hoping to gain the co-operation of Vichy France against Britain and could not start dismembering its colonial empire. The French Empire was also showing disturbing signs of defecting to General Charles de Gaulle's Free French movement and handing over part of it to Spain might precipitate this defection, which would open up the Atlantic and Mediterranean coasts of north-west Africa to the British and Americans. Hitler's interview with Pétain, ruler of Vichy France, was more agreeable than his talks with Franco, but no more productive. Hitler had even less to offer the French, largely because any strengthening of the French position in Africa would have upset Mussolini.

Mussolini was the central figure in Hitler's Mediterranean strategy. Hitler urged on his fellow-dictator to attack the British in Egypt. In the summer of 1940 the British were much inferior to the Italians in manpower and might have succumbed to a determined

Spain and Vichy France unable to assist Hitler in the Med -iterranean

87

Italian attack across the 350 miles of desert from the Italian colony of Libya. Hitler offered assistance, but Mussolini's pride demanded that the victory should be won by the Italians on their own, and he turned the promised aid down. As the months went by, nothing decisive happened, as the Italian general in command insisted that the army was not yet ready. Yet Mussolini was desperate for military glory and unwilling to wait any longer. If preparations in North Africa were incomplete, he was open to suggestions about achieving glory elsewhere. In practice, the only other possible area of Italian expansion was the Balkans. Conquests there, like conquests in Egypt, would help him towards his underlying aim of recreating the Roman Empire and converting the Mediterranean into *mare nostrum* (our sea) once more.

Italian ambitions in the Balkans

2. The Campaign in Greece and Crete

Mussolini regarded the Balkans as coming within his sphere of influence and had at various times contemplated action against Yugoslavia or Greece. The Germans, however, were keen that peace in the Balkans should be preserved, in case the Soviets found in turmoil there an excuse for intervention. In mid-September 1940 Mussolini discovered that the Germans had made an agreement with Romania to station troops there. The country was important to Italy as the source of its oil and the Duce was furious that the Germans had acted, without even consulting him beforehand. He determined to surprise Hitler with an action of his own, the invasion of Greece. He acted out of pique, but also with a view to enhancing his prestige among the Italian people, who needed to see that he did not always play second fiddle to Hitler.

Mussolini fixed the attack on Greece for 28 October. Everyone who mattered in Italy was convinced that the war against the Greeks would be a walkover, which is presumably the reason why the Italians thought they could risk an invasion so late in the year. The weather

Mussolini attacks Greece Oct 1940

certainly contributed to the disaster that overwhelmed the Italians. The rain and the mud bogged down the Italian tanks and heavy guns. The poor roads became impassable. Naval operations were hampered by stormy seas and the air force could not function properly in the fog. The Italians were short of everything: men, fuel, ammunition. They were surprised to find themselves fighting determined and better organized enemies who made the most of their local knowledge of the difficult terrain. The Italian attack ground to a halt after a week or so and the Greeks were able to push the Italians back well within the Albanian border, the Italians' starting point.

Italian offensive fails

In 1939 the British had given Greece a guarantee and Mussolini's aggression triggered a British obligation to come to its aid. The Greeks feared that if they accepted aid, they might do themselves more harm than good by causing Hitler to intervene on Mussolini's side. Anthony Eden, however, backed a policy of intervention when sent to assess the situation and General Wavell, the British commander in Egypt, thought that success in Greece would be useful, in that it would prevent German intervention in the Mediterranean by way of the Aegean. Hence, when the Greeks changed their minds about seeking British aid, the British government responded positively. Forces were diverted from Egypt, but inevitably they were limited in numbers and equipment, since Britain's top priority was the defence of Egypt and the Canal. Hitler had decided that he dared not risk the British entrenching themselves in Greece, which was much too close to the Romanian oilfields, on which he was so heavily dependent. In April 1941 his forces invaded Yugoslavia and Greece just as the British were landing in Greece. The Greeks wholly lacked the modern equipment which might have enabled them to resist the Germans. Attacks came from three directions at once, including Yugoslavia, which collapsed in only a week. British forces were inadequate and never co-operated properly with the Greek armies. The war had not lasted 24 days when the British re-embarked their troops.

German forces invade Yugoslavia and Greece

British
and Greek
defence of
Crete

The British made a more serious effort to hang on to Crete, which could have provided them with useful airbases and denied them to the Germans. Over 26,000 Commonwealth troops and about as many Greek soldiers held the island in May 1941. They expected attack, but assumed that it would come by sea. The Royal Navy proved too powerful for a sea-borne attack to be possible and the Germans therefore relied entirely on an air-borne invasion. At 8 am on 20 May, 3,000 troops were parachuted into Crete and captured one of the airfields. Over the next hours and days the Germans built up their forces to about 22,000 men, who arrived by parachute, glider and troop-carrier. These were well-trained, tough fighters who had the advantage that the Luftwaffe dominated the air. By the 26 May the British decided to withdraw their troops. The Royal Navy rescued two thirds of them, though it suffered badly from air attacks in the process.

Hitler fails
to capitalize
on Med-
iterranean
victories

The Greek campaign seemed at the time a total disaster. Troops had been diverted from North Africa and had achieved nothing at all. Fortunately, Hitler was not interested in following up his victories. The Führer rejected advice to seize Cyprus and from there to strike at the Suez Canal. Since the Royal Navy, however battered, still controlled the seas, the proposed attacks could only have been made by air and Hitler was aware that Germany had paid a high price for its victory in Crete, where 4,000 picked troops had been killed and half as many wounded. He was therefore unwilling to sanction more air-borne invasions. Besides, his attention was wholly absorbed by his forthcoming war with the USSR.

3. The Italian Collapse in Africa

In the second half of 1940, the Italians seemed in a strong position in eastern Africa. British forces in the area were small, only 9,000 in the Sudan and a little fewer in Kenya. By contrast, Italian forces in the region amounted to 91,000 together with at least 100,000 native troops. The Italians used their superiority to occupy some frontier posts in the Sudan and to overrun British Somaliland, from where they came to pose a threat to British sea traffic entering the Red Sea from the south. Their main weakness in the Horn of Africa was their isolation. There was no hope of reinforcement or of additional supplies of munitions or motor fuel. The Italians could not count either on the loyalty of their subjects, particularly in Abyssinia (now Ethiopia), where their regime was newly established and brutal. Once the British built up their forces, the result of the war in the Horn of Africa could not long remain in doubt, though the British were surprised by the speed of the Italian collapse in Somaliland and most of Abyssinia. By May 1941 the main Italian commander was down to a few thousand troops and could see no alternative to surrender. Nearly a quarter of a million Italian troops altogether had become prisoners of war and Mussolini's East African empire had been lost.

In Libya, however, the Italians looked better placed. Hundreds of thousands of troops faced 36,000 British, New Zealand and Indian soldiers guarding Egypt, and here it was the British who had communications problems. Italian power in the Mediterranean made it dangerous to use the sea-route through the Mediterranean, and the British took to using the very long and slow route via the Cape in South Africa. In the years immediately before the war, however, the British had taken pains to create mobile forces whose members had mastered the techniques of driving and navigating in the desert, who could maintain their vehicles and equipment despite the ever-present grit and dust and the frequent sandstorms and who had learnt how to use the terrain for movement and concealment. They thus had a qualitative advantage which partially offset their deficiency in numbers.

Italians in Libya

In September 1940 the Italians advanced from Libya as far as Sidi Barrani, where they stopped in order to make sure of their supply links to the west. While they were there, established in a chain of fortified camps, Wavell planned Operation Compass, designed as a large-scale

Operation Compass

91

raid to disrupt Italian preparations for a further advance. He had recently been reinforced by a tank regiment equipped with the Matilda, a 26-ton tank, which was slow, but very heavily armoured, and so impervious to all Italian anti-tank weapons. His air support had been updated too. The carefully planned operation in December achieved surprise in its opening phase and took advantage of the Italian mistake in placing their camps too far apart for mutual support, so that they could be overcome one at a time. Within three days, the entire Italian position in and around Sidi Barrani had been overrun. Tens of thousands of prisoners and large numbers of tanks, guns and transport vehicles had been captured, while those killed or wounded on the British side amounted to a few hundred.

Defeat of Italians at Sidi Barrani

The British could not at once follow up their unexpected success, because Wavell had to send some of the victorious troops to deal with the Italians in the Horn of Africa and adequate replacements were not available for a while. There were supply problems too, now that the army was so far forward of its prepared depots. New depots had to be stocked with petrol and water brought up by motor vehicle and ship. Captured Italian transport and supplies proved invaluable. At last, in early January 1941, the British were ready to move on the port of Bardia, just inside Libya, and after it fell, on the strongly fortified port of Tobruk, another 75 miles westwards along the coast. The Australians prepared their attack meticulously, using aerial reconnaissance to acquire a detailed knowledge of the Italian defensive system, which enabled them to devise methods of overcoming it. Aided by bombardment from the sea and the air, Australian forces took the town in attacks on 21 and 22 January. The British had still not finished. When the opportunity occurred to cut off the Italian army retreating from the eastern province of Cyrenaica, they took it and at Beda Fomm a small British force with only a few tanks secured the surrender of a force many times its own size.

Australians take Tobruk

Some British commanders were anxious to follow up their success and clear the Italians out of North Africa altogether. They were, however, commanded to halt their advance. One reason for this order was the diversion of troops and equipment to Greece, and it has often been claimed that the British threw away a golden opportunity in favour of an ill-thought-out adventure to the north. It is by no means certain that a great opportunity was missed. Practically everything the British used, from tanks to uniforms, was worn out after covering such large distances in such severe conditions. The Italians were falling back on their supplies, but the British were moving away from theirs. So far luck had been with the British, but they could hardly continue to rely on it. There had at least to be a pause in the headlong advance. During the pause a new and formidable enemy joined the fray.

4. The Intervention of the Afrikakorps

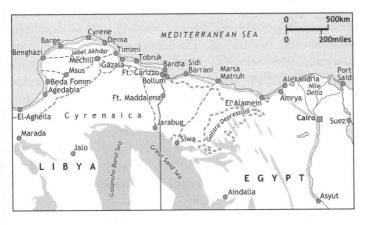

NORTH AFRICA, 1941-3

Learning of the disasters that had befallen the Italians in north Africa, Hitler decided that Tripolitania at least had to be held and he determined to send to Africa a force which became known as

Rommel and the Afrikakorps

the Afrikakorps. Erwin Rommel was chosen to command it. Rommel had proved a successful commander of a Panzer regiment in the war of 1940 against France, though he had quarrelled with his peers and superiors in the army: they disliked his arrogance and tendency to disregard orders and to take excessive risks. Once in Africa from February 1941, he overrode the plans of the Italian generals, who were nominally in control, and hustled his own subordinates into taking the offensive as soon as possible. He was thus able to catch the British off balance, since they had assumed that he would take months to organize his forces. Yet the main factor in his favour was the lack of British forces in Cyrenaica. The area was not yet a priority for Wavell or the British government. Their troops were fighting in Greece and the Horn of Africa, and Egypt and the Canal did not seem to be in any danger. Rommel was therefore able to push the British back to the Egyptian border with very little trouble, except that Wavell ordered an Australian division to dig in at Tobruk. The defence of the port was dogged and skilful. Rommel seems to have been over-confident, assuming that the Australians would crumble when confronted with his Panzers and harried from above by his Stuka dive-bombers. He does not appear to have prepared his attacks with the sort of care which the British had shown when they had attacked the Italians in Tobruk a few months earlier. Hence his forces proved inadequate to overcome the defenders. In two major attacks more than half of Rommel's tanks were disabled and he had no option but to end his attacks and settle for a lengthy siege. The stalwart defence of Tobruk became a symbol of the British will to resist. Goebbels, the Nazi Propaganda Minister, contemptuously referred to the defenders as rats, whereupon the British forces in North Africa proudly took to calling themselves the 'Desert Rats'.

Lack of British forces in Cyrenaica

Defence of Tobruk

'Desert Rats'

Rommel's main weakness during 1941 was inadequate supplies. He needed 50,000 tons a day to maintain his forces and to build up some reserves for serious offensive operations. He was enormously handicapped by the need to bring supplies along the thousand-mile overland route from Tripoli, which meant that many of the supplies of food, petrol and so on were consumed simply in getting them to the Afrikakorps. Tobruk would have been valuable as a handy port for landing supplies needed for an attack upon Egypt. Getting supplies to Tripoli was not easy either. The Royal Navy continued to be powerful in the Mediterranean, even though it was challenged by air power. The Italian Navy was worsted in air and sea attacks, and usually kept out of the way. The British had developed the island of Malta as a base for squadrons of fighters and bombers, which took a fearful toll of Italian and German shipping: in 1941 perhaps 60 per cent of it was sunk. Apart from these difficulties, Hitler and the Army High Command did not accord a high priority to Rommel's operations in Africa: the lion's share of resources went to the war against the USSR, which had started in June 1941. In these circumstances, the best Rommel's forces could do was to thwart various British efforts to relieve Tobruk in the spring of 1941.

In contrast to the Germans, the British government under Churchill thought the North African campaigns important, since after the fall of Greece they could strike at Germany only there. British forces in Egypt were built up in preference to those in the Far East, where the situation looked increasingly menacing as 1941 went on. Disappointed by British defeats at Rommel's hands, in June Churchill replaced Wavell with Auchinleck as the commander of British forces in the Middle East, though he was soon disappointed with Auchinleck's caution. Auchinleck realized that his troops were exhausted and their morale was low. The Panzers were superior to the British tanks and German anti-tank weapons had become devastatingly effective. He did not feel ready to launch his counter-stroke against Rommel, Operation Crusader, until mid-November 1941. Whatever the quality of Rommel's weaponry, that of the British was far superior in quantity. When Crusader began, the German general took the reckless decision to strike at the British rear units and

Superiority of Panzer troops

their lines of communication with Egypt. Auchinleck refused to panic and Rommel's stroke was soon revealed as bluff. Few of his tanks had kept up with him and he was disastrously short of supplies. Rommel had shot his bolt. He proceeded to lose almost all of the gains he had made earlier in the year. Tobruk was relieved; most of Cyrenaica was brought back under British control.

Operation Crusader

Operation Crusader had the same ending as Operation Compass nearly a year previously. Once again, attacking Axis forces had outrun their supplies and been forced back into Tripolitania. The likelihood was, however, that the new British advance would suffer the same fate that the advance of 1940-41 had suffered. On the western borders of Cyrenaica the British were once again far from their supplies, whereas Rommel was again close to his. Besides, the British had paid dearly for their victory. Their losses were fewer than those of the Axis, but still amounted to 15 per cent of the troops engaged. The morale of the troops seems not to have been raised by their victory. A cynical scepticism about their own generals contrasted with an admiration for Rommel, who was regarded as the one brilliant military commander of the war. His reputation was about to be still further enhanced.

5. The Turn of the Tide: the Battles of El Alamein

It was clear to Hitler and his advisors that adequate supplies were the key to success in North Africa. There were two main obstacles to building up supplies there. The first was the Royal Navy. Late in 1941 twenty-five U-boats were sent to the Mediterranean to reduce the

Sinking of the *Ark Royal*

Royal Navy's dominance. They succeeded in sinking a British aircraft-carrier, HMS *Ark Royal*. The other was the island of Malta, which functioned as an unsinkable aircraft-carrier from where the British wrought havoc with Axis shipping. Malta could not be sunk, but it could be bombed. At the end of 1941 German military aircraft were based on Sicily under the command of Field Marshal Kesselring and from the last few days of December Malta was subjected to a relentless bombing campaign which steadily increased in intensity until in May 1942 Kesselring could assert, 'There is nothing left to bomb.' On 15 April George VI awarded the whole community of the island the George Cross to bear witness to its 'heroism and devotion'. The RAF on Malta continued to function, but Kesselring's bombardment did enable supplies to get through to Rommel. The most important convoy arrived in January with 54 of the best German tanks as well as armoured cars and anti-tank guns. The tanks joined the existing 84 tanks of the Afrikakorps and as many again Italian tanks. Through the spring there were ample deliveries of food and fuel too.

Bombing of Malta

Rommel's reinforcements made possible a fresh attempt to shake the British hold on the Middle East, but his force was basically far too small for the job. At first this underlying reality was concealed by Rommel's boldness and British ineptitude. At the start of 1942 he took the widely scattered and mostly inexperienced British formations by surprise and drove them in headlong retreat back towards the Egyptian frontier. The British retreat was halted for some weeks at the Gazala line, but at the end of May a new attack by Rommel produced a fresh retreat by the British army and the surrender of Tobruk. With Tobruk were lost 33,000 men together with 2,000 serviceable vehicles and huge quantities of guns, ammunition, food and petrol. Back in Europe, Hitler was delighted and at once promoted Rommel to field marshal. The victory appeared to open the way to the conquest of Egypt and Hitler agreed to back Rommel in a further advance to the Nile rather than mount the planned Operation Hercules, an invasion of Malta. Had the latter gone ahead, it could well have succeeded, given that the Royal Navy in the area was so severely depleted by a retreat from Alexandria, now considered too vulnerable, and the dispatch of reinforcements to the Far East. If Malta had fallen, the Axis supply route to Africa would have been secure and the chances of eventual success in Africa much greater. In Britain the heroic defence of Tobruk in 1941 had accustomed people to thinking of it as a vital strongpoint. There was intense anger and

British surrender Tobruk June 1942

alarm when it fell and a motion of no confidence in Churchill's government was moved in the Commons, though it did not succeed.

Rommel's victory was not what it seemed to him and to his foes. British mistakes and confusion and his own boldness and skill could not forever disguise the truth that Rommel lacked the means to achieve his goal. By the start of July he had only 1,500 infantry and 55 tanks. His men had reached the limit of endurance and, despite the supplies captured at Tobruk, Rommel was desperately short of petrol, ammunition, food and water. The British, by contrast, had all that they needed, since they were so close to their bases. Many of their troops were fresh and their air force had been reinforced. When Rommel attacked again at El Alamein, the British units stood firm and fought bravely. It was enough to stop the German advance at last.

First Battle of El Alamein July 1942

Early in August Churchill and Sir Alan Brooke, the Chief of the Imperial General Staff, flew to Egypt to assess the situation. They were appalled by the demoralised state of the army and resolved upon a change of leadership. Auchinleck was replaced as Commander-in-Chief Middle East by Sir Harold Alexander, while Bernard Montgomery was to lead the Eighth Army. Montgomery exuded confidence, ending all talk of further retreat and issuing clear orders that the next German attack was to be resisted to the utmost on the line which the troops occupied. By the end of August Rommel had rebuilt his forces, though he remained critically short of petrol. He launched one more attack which he hoped might force his opponents into another retreat, but at Alam Halfa the British army stood up to his onslaught and he was forced to withdraw. The British Army began to suspect that the tide had turned at last and their confidence in their new commander was confirmed.

Montgomery commander of Eighth Army

In London Churchill was desperate for a great victory, but Montgomery insisted on careful preparation and it was seven weeks before he went on the offensive against Rommel. British superiority was greater than ever before: over 200,000 men against 60,000 Germans and Italians; 1200 tanks against 260 German tanks; 1200 aeroplanes against about 350. The Germans were critically short of petrol and food and poor hygiene in the trenches had led to the spread of dysentery and jaundice. Rommel himself fell ill and missed the start of Montgomery's attack. The Germans fought hard at the Second Battle of El Alamein, but the result was never in serious doubt. The overwhelming numerical and material superiority of the British was bound to tell. By 2 November Rommel was compelled to sound the retreat. He could do no more than attempt to save as much of the Afrikakorps as possible. For Churchill the news of the victory came as a blessed relief. 'It is not the beginning of the end, but it may be the end of the beginning,' he declared.

Second Battle of El Alamein October 1942

6. The Expulsion of the Axis from Africa

Churchill was right in suggesting that in the second half of 1942 the fortunes of war had begun to change. The victory of El Alamein was affected by two significant factors. First, in the summer of 1942 Malta was relieved, especially by the arrival of a large convoy in mid-August with food and aviation fuel. The air forces based there were reorganised by Keith Park, of Battle of Britain fame, and a large number of Spitfires were delivered. The Luftwaffe began to suffer heavy losses and its attacks on the island became less severe. The British attack on Axis shipping in the central Mediterranean became devastatingly effective, as submarines, bombers and torpedo bombers sent two thirds of Italy's merchant marine to the sea-bed. The impact on Rommel's forces was great: half the supplies sent to them never arrived; above all, they were denied two thirds of the petrol dispatched to them. The Mediterranean was becoming a British lake once more.

Relief of Malta

A second, even more ominous development influenced the outcome at El Alamein. The tank force under Montgomery included large numbers of American tanks, Grants and Shermans, equipped with powerful 75mm guns. These were much the best tanks on the British side, equal to the best that Rommel had and much more

Grant and Sherman tanks

numerous. Nearly a year after the USA had officially joined in the war, American industrial might was beginning to tell. The Germans were about to be treated to an even more spectacular exhibition of American power.

The Americans were anxious not simply to provide their allies with equipment, but to strike at Germany themselves. Only with difficulty did the British persuade them that a cross-Channel invasion of Nazi Europe in 1942 was impracticable. Churchill worked on Roosevelt and gradually convinced him that a campaign in North Africa would prove successful and useful. Some American statesmen continued to think that Churchill was more concerned with utility for the British Empire than with utility to the cause of overthrowing Hitler, but the USA became committed to Operation Torch. The plan was to take control in French North Africa, where local French authorities might well prove friendly, and then move on to Tunisia to link up with Montgomery, who would be chasing Rommel westwards. The Axis could then be expelled from Africa and what Churchill called the 'soft under-belly' of Nazi Europe would be exposed. Perhaps the most striking aspect of Operation Torch was its demonstration of American reach. On 8th November 1942 a fleet of nearly 700 ships, accompanied by five battleships and seven aircraft carriers, landed 63,000 men and 430 tanks at three points on the Mediterranean coast of Morocco and Algeria. Half the force came directly from America, the other half from Scotland.

Operation Torch

In most ways Torch turned out well. The authorities in French North Africa were mostly co-operative: it helped that Hitler chose this moment to snuff out the last shred of French independence by occupying Vichy France. Spain did not interfere with Allied operations. The remaining Axis forces were soon bottled up in the area of Tunis. Rommel went to see both Mussolini and Hitler to urge the evacuation of their forces from Africa before it was too late. Hoping to avoid this humiliation and misled by the successes of the resistance to the onslaught of the British under Montgomery and the

German occupation of Vichy France

Americans under General Eisenhower, the dictators turned down his pleas. Whatever military skill the Germans might display, their eventual failure was certain, because of the dominance of the sea and the air which Britain had come to exercise. The Axis forces needed well over 100,000 tons of supplies per month, but in March and again in April they received under 30,000 tons. Food, ammunition and equipment of all kinds were running out. The final surrender in May 1943 became inevitable.

The folly of Hitler and Mussolini in rejecting Rommel's advice to evacuate their forces now became clear. Up to 150,000 Axis troops were taken into captivity, including very large numbers of battle-hardened veterans. The victorious Allies were elated by their success: British belief in eventual victory was fully restored. The Allies had now to decide what to do with their victory.

Rommel's surrender May 1943

7. The Allied Invasion of Italy

General Marshall, Chief of the American Army Staff, remained desperate to launch a cross-Channel invasion and was suspicious of any plans which appeared to divert Allied efforts from that enterprise. The British were keen to extend their Mediterranean strategy while they still could. At a conference in Casablanca Sir Alan Brooke, Chief of Imperial General Staff, proposed an invasion of Sicily, which would make the Mediterranean much safer for Allied shipping and perhaps force Mussolini out of the war. The British got their way and in July 1943 the invasion of Sicily duly went ahead.

General Marshall

Allied invasion of Sicily July 1943

Coastal landings are usually the most difficult part of such military operations, but the Sicilians manning the coastal defences had little interest in dying for Mussolini and realised that the sooner they surrendered, the less damage would be done to their homes. The burden of defending the island in fact fell more or less entirely on the 33,000 German troops stationed on the island together with as many again who reinforced them. Making skilful use of the terrain, they

THE WAR IN EUROPE:
The Western Front,
the Mediterranean
and Middle East Front
and the Eastern Front

delayed the inevitable victory of the 450,000 Allied troops. On the Allied side, there were bitter quarrels between the two tactless and egotistical commanders, Montgomery and the American George Patton, whose main concern sometimes seemed to be to race each other into Messina, the last redoubt of the German forces. The island fell in 38 days, but the success was marred by the successful evacuation of the German forces with most of their equipment. Perhaps because the Allied leaders had not yet decided what they should do after the conquest of Sicily, no attempt was made to block the German retreat by landing forces in Calabria, the toe of Italy.

While the conquest of Sicily was proceeding, the foundations of Mussolini's power were crumbling away. Since the defeat of El Alamein, Italian enthusiasm for fighting at Germany's side had waned and Mussolini's one-time popularity had disappeared. On 24 July the Fascist Grand Council passed a vote of no confidence in him and the next day the King sacked him and appointed Marshal Badoglio in his

Mussolini arrested

stead. Mussolini was arrested. The immediate reaction in Italy was one of joy and everywhere Fascist emblems were torn down. The new government initiated secret negotiations with the Allies for an armistice, but the Germans had for months suspected that Italy might attempt to switch sides. German troops under Rommel's command were sent into northern Italy to secure the mountain passes and crucial roads and railways. In the south Kesselring made preparations in case Italy repudiated its alliance with Germany.

In August 1943 the decision to invade Italy was taken by the Allies.

Allies invade Italian mainland September 1943

In early September there were landings by Montgomery in the toe of Italy, with a further landing in the heel and the main landing in the Bay of Salerno under the American general Mark Clark. When Eisenhower announced the armistice, in the hope of neutralising the Italian army, the Germans swiftly reacted. They disarmed the Italians and occupied the main cities. The King and the Italian government, which had done nothing to forestall such an eventuality, fled to the protection of the Allies at Brindisi, in the boot of Italy. The Germans announced the formation of a new Fascist government and then rescued Mussolini from confinement in order to make him head of the new Italian Social Republic. He had no independence of Germany and the parts of Italy which acknowledged him were treated like the rest of occupied Europe as a source of goods and labour. Mussolini himself rarely left his villa on Lake Garda and was treated with contempt by the Fuhrer.

It had been fondly hoped by leaders such as Churchill that an invasion of Italy might expose the 'soft under-belly' of Nazi-Europe. This prospect proved to be an illusion. The terrain in Italy gave innumerable opportunities for effective defensive warfare and the Germans skilfully availed themselves of them. Progress northwards through Italy proved agonisingly slow. By the end of the first month after the landings, about a third of mainland Italy was in Allied hands. It took another year to secure the next third and hopes of finally attacking into Austria seemed by then merely fanciful. In the end, Italy was secured by the capitulation of the Germans in the country, less than a week before the surrender of Germany itself. By then a formidable Resistance movement, often led by Communists, had arisen in Italy, and with the German surrender, they were able to seize control in many places in northern Italy. Mussolini and his mistress were captured and shot by partisans of the Resistance. Their corpses were strung up in a Milanese square, where they were kicked and spat upon by the mob.

Mussolini shot by partisans April 1945

For a long time, Italy had been a sideshow. Events elsewhere were much more important in bringing about Hitler's downfall.

VI

THE DOWNFALL OF THE THIRD REICH

1. The Battle of the Atlantic

IT seems to have been Churchill who christened the Battle of the Atlantic in a speech of March 1941, when he identified it as 'the real issue of the war' for Britain. He was referring to the German

U-boats and control of the Atlantic submarine or U-boat attacks on the flow of supplies to Britain from overseas and the attempt of Britain to defeat their attack. Half of Britain's food and two thirds of its requirements of raw materials came from abroad. The Atlantic link with the United States was particularly vital, even before it entered the war, as the products of American industry were increasingly made available to Britain's war effort. Once America did become an ally at the end of 1941, any joint action against Hitler and his allies depended upon control of the Atlantic sea crossings. It was perhaps not quite true to say that if Hitler achieved control of the sea, he would win, since he needed to subdue a great land power, the USSR. But it was certainly true that if Britain and America lost that control, then Britain would be finished and America would be unable to land any blows on Hitler. It is not surprising that Churchill later wrote, 'The only thing that ever really frightened me during the war was the U-boat peril.'

The statistics show why Churchill became worried. In 1940 the German U-boat effort was only half-hearted, in that the Germans rarely had much more than a dozen U-boats in the crucial area of the Atlantic and still they succeeded in sinking 4 million tons of shipping, a quarter of the British merchant marine. They had broken the British naval codes and so knew where the convoys were and they evaded the sound-detecting equipment of the convoy escorts by attacking on the surface at night. When a convoy was sighted, brief radio transmissions called the U-boats to form a 'wolf pack' for the attack. During 1941 the British had some successes in their battle against the U-boats: they broke the German codes and thereby were able to discover where the U-boats were and route convoys away from danger, and much better air cover for convoys was provided. Yet as the Germans realized what the U-boats were achieving, they steadily increased the number of U-boats towards the total of 300 regarded by their commander Admiral Donitz as the optimum, and by the end of the year the tonnage of shipping lost was still increasing.

The year 1942 was the worst in the Battle of the Atlantic. The Germans broke the Allied codes again and so knew the routes of the convoys, whereas they changed their own codes and deprived the Allies of information about the U-boats. The Germans built 'milch-cows', submarines of exceptional size which were used to refuel smaller U-boats, so that they needed to return to base less frequently and could spend longer hunting convoys. Yet the U-boats did not have things all their own way. Their greatest enemy was the aeroplane and vast areas of the Atlantic were patrolled from Northern Ireland, Iceland and Newfoundland. There remained an 'Atlantic Gap' in the middle of the ocean beyond the range of Allied aircraft and it was here that Donitz concentrated his U-boats. Sinkings in the Atlantic totalled 5.4 million tons, an unsustainable rate of loss. British imports declined to a third of their 1938 level and oil stocks were reduced to a critically low level.

The 'Atlantic Gap'

Yet developments were already taking place that were ominous for the future of the U-boat offensive. Radar and the powerful searchlights with which Allied aircraft were increasingly equipped helped them to detect the position of U-boats, while improved aerial depth-charges made it more possible to destroy them. For escort ships new centimetric radar and a multiple mortar performed the same tasks. Losses of U-boats began steadily to rise, while the tonnage sunk by each operating U-boat fell.

In 1943 the Germans further stepped up the U-boat war and unprecedented numbers of U-boats operated in the Atlantic Gap. The

British government had appointed Admiral Sir Max Horton as Commander-in-Chief of the Western Approaches. He set in train the acquisition of long-range aircraft to fill the Gap. He insisted on longer and better training of convoy escorts. The changes he made could not take immediate effect and there were near-catastrophic losses in the early months of the year, despite the fact that the British were able again to decrypt the German codes. By April, however, Horton was confident enough to drive convoys in amongst the waiting U-boats. Trained escorts, long-range aircraft and lurking support groups of destroyers and escort (aircraft) carriers then set about the U-boats. There was a particularly satisfactory outcome when in May convoy SC130 sailed from Nova Scotia to England and six U-boats were sunk for no loss at all among the convoy. May 1943 was the turning point in the battle against the U-boats. Sinkings in the North Atlantic fell to 160,000 tons and 41 U-boats were lost. At the end of the month Donitz had to report to Hitler that the Battle of the Atlantic was lost for the moment.

Turning point in Battle of the Atlantic May 1943

It turned out that the Battle was lost for good. Donitz did try again in the later part of 1943, but his losses were crippling. In the last seven months of 1943, 141 U-boats were lost in order to sink only 57 Allied ships. In the whole of 1944 only 170,000 tons of Allied shipping were lost, a mere 3 per cent of the losses suffered in 1942. By then Donitz had nearly 400 U-boats, but they rarely dared to emerge from their home ports. The shift from near-defeat to victory had occurred quite suddenly in the spring of 1943. It was the product not of one decisive factor, but of the coming together of many which in combination had turned the tables on the U-boats. The organiser of victory was Admiral Horton, but he depended not only on the sea captains, sailors and pilots, but also on the cryptanalysts at Bletchley Park, the meticulous trackers of the U-boats in the Tracking Room and the inventors who kept refining radar and means of delivering bombs from aeroplanes and surface vessels.

Bletchley Park code breakers

Men did not die in huge masses in the U-boat war, as they did on the Russian Front, but the cumulative loss of life was great. Of 39,000

German submariners, 28,000 perished. Over 55,000 crew-members went down with British merchant ships; nearly half of them were drowned. The outcome of the Battle in which these men perished was decisive for the outcome of the Second World War as a whole. Complete control of the sea was one of the factors that made possible what Hitler in 1940 had not dared to attempt, an amphibious landing on a hostile shore, that of Normandy.

2. Hitler's War against the Soviet Union: the Failure of Operation Barbarossa

By the time the Anglo-American forces landed in Normandy in 1944, Hitler's Germany had already been gravely weakened by its struggle with the Soviet Union. Hitler had decided on the war in December 1940 and during the first half of 1941 his attention was focused on preparations for it. His original plan was to begin the offensive in May, but the need to extricate Mussolini from his Balkan adventure caused a six-week postponement to 22 June. When his great enterprise miscarried, Hitler blamed Mussolini because of this delay, but atrocious weather in the relevant area of Europe would probably have imposed delay in any case. In invading the USSR with Britain undefeated behind him, Hitler raised the spectre of war on two fronts, so repeating the error of Imperial Germany. Hope of averting this danger seems to have motivated Hitler's deputy Rudolf Hess in his bizarre and unauthorized flight to Scotland in May 1941. He hoped that through the Duke of Hamilton, whom he wrongly believed to be politically significant, he might be able to deliver peace with Britain to a grateful Fuhrer. Hess soon began a life in prison, first in Britain, later in post-war Germany, which lasted till 1987. He achieved nothing beyond profound embarrassment for Hitler.

Hess in Scotland May 1941

The attack on the USSR was Hitler's greatest gamble yet. He staked everything on achieving in Russia the same kind of victory that he had achieved with such ease in France. To this end, he had doubled the number of Panzer divisions; he also doubled the number of half-track vehicles, which made a large part of the infantry mobile so that they could hold the ground overrun by the tanks. Yet the USSR was a much more formidable foe than France. The population of the state was at least 170 million, more than double that of Germany. The Germans had already mobilized all their prime manpower, but the Soviets had millions of reservists. Moreover, the USSR was huge. In France the Germans had been able to supply their army with lorries plying between the army and the German border, but such lorries had a range of only 300km. In Russia this was nowhere near enough, as the Germans realized. They hoped to extend their supply system 500km into the USSR by having one set of lorries shuttling between the border and intermediate dumps and another set shuttling between the intermediate dumps and the armies. Beyond 500km, the line of the Dvina-Dnieper Rivers, the Wehrmacht would be in very serious logistical trouble. This was particularly the case because the Soviet railway system was difficult to use – because of its narrow gauge and, it turned out, Russian expertise in demolition – and inadequate. All these considerations pointed to the paramount need to destroy the Soviet armies and the Soviet state west of the Dvina-Dnieper Rivers. If the Germans failed in this, they would be sucked into a war of attrition which it would be near-impossible for them to win, especially since they had not finished off their Western enemies.

Logistical difficulties in supplying German troops

It had taken Germany three years to knock Russia out of the First World War. In 1941 Hitler expected to do the job in less than six months. The Germans knew that under Stalin the USSR had become a great industrial power. They were certain, however, that the Soviet army would disintegrate under the onslaught of the Wehrmacht. Since the fall of France, confidence in the Wehrmacht had become absolute, while Stalin's army purges of 1937-8 and the inglorious Soviet war of 1939-40 against Finland suggested that the Red Army would not prove a difficult opponent.

The Germans attacked on 22 June, launching a campaign named Operation Barbarossa (Red-beard) after a medieval crusading Emperor. The Soviet forces were taken by surprise, since Stalin had refused to believe all the intelligence which pointed to an imminent German attack. In the first days of the war huge numbers of prisoners were taken and vast quantities of Soviet military equipment were destroyed. In early July it seemed to some Germans that the war was as good as won. A few weeks later, they were less sure. The Soviet armies were still fighting, with ever more fanatical intensity as the intentions of the Germans to kill or enslave the population became clear. Faster than divisions could be destroyed, new ones were constituted. By late July the German advance towards Moscow was slowed to a near-halt by predictable logistical problems. The successes of the Wehrmacht, however, had not yet come to an end. Hitler swung his forces into the Ukraine, encircling Kiev and taking two thirds of a million prisoners. Meanwhile, in the north Leningrad was surrounded. Then Operation Typhoon against Moscow began. In early October the German armies were a mere hundred kilometres from Moscow.

Operation Barbarossa June 1941

Operation Typhoon

The Germans had reached their high-water mark. Autumn rains which turned the countryside into a quagmire and winter cold against which no preparations had been made had disastrous effects on the German armies. The supply problems now that they were 1000km beyond the frontier were very serious. Quite apart from transport problems, German supplies of petrol were very low. In December 1941, for the first time, the Soviet armies under Marshal Zhukov took the initiative, achieved surprise and inflicted defeat on the German Army Group Centre. For a moment, catastrophe stared the Germans in the face, but Stalin let them off the hook by insisting on a premature advance all along the front, instead of concentrating at the point where the Germans had been knocked off balance. Yet things were bad enough. German losses had been huge, 750,000 or more. The Red Army had not been destroyed. There loomed the

Marshal Zhukov

war of attrition which Germany could not win. The Germans still had not got their hands on the raw material resources which they needed to continue the war with any prospect of success.

3. Failure Again: the Disaster of Stalingrad

The last month of 1941 brought Hitler good news as well as bad. Japan turned its forces southwards against the United States and the British Empire. Just before the attack on the US at Pearl Harbor, Japan had signed an alliance with Germany, promising not to make a separate peace with the USA. Hitler duly declared war on the USA after receiving news of Pearl Harbor. For him, this formal declaration made little difference. In August 1941 Churchill and Roosevelt had met at Placentia Bay, Newfoundland. The chief outcome was the Atlantic Charter, whereby both countries committed themselves to the right of nations to determine their own future, but Britain had gained American co-operation in the war against the U-boats. In Hitler's view, Britain and the USA were virtually allied against Germany already. He foresaw great advantages to Germany in the war of Japan against the Western powers. They would be tied up in a Pacific war and unable to concentrate on Germany. Perhaps Britain would at last see how disastrous its war with Germany was and seek to extricate itself in order to salvage what it could of the Empire. If all went to plan, Germany would have another year in which to finish off the Soviet Union.

German alliance with Japan 1941

The Atlantic Charter

Hitler's calculations were awry in many respects. He wholly failed to appreciate the loathing for him so widely felt in Britain, which ruled out any possibility of peace. 'Right or wrong', Hitler said to Goebbels, 'we must win...And once we have won, who is going to question our methods?' Fortunately, we do not know what might have happened if Hitler had won, but while he was still trying to win, his brutal methods were a gift to Allied propaganda, even though some of the worst atrocities of the extermination camps set up to murder the Jews were not yet public knowledge. Hitler also failed fully to appreciate the awesome power of the United States. No more than Germany was Japan a world power and the USA was quite capable of dealing with both at once.

Yet perhaps Hitler's most serious miscalculation was his underestimation of the Red Army. In the early months of 1942, though, the German Army seemed to justify Hitler's confidence in it. Attacks by the Red Army were beaten off and significant progress was made in the south of Russia. The main aim of Operation Blue in 1942 was to conquer the oilfields of the Caucasus and end for ever the shortages which had proved crippling before Moscow the previous December. Hitler did not, however, concentrate all his forces on that ambitious objective and he sent his Sixth Army towards Stalingrad, a city on the Volga which was a key distribution point for supplies to and from the Caucasus and bore the name of the leader against whom Hitler's armies were fighting. The troops of General Paulus first entered the city in the first half of September, but it proved difficult to subdue the entire urban centre. Both sides decided to fight for the city to the death, conferring on it a symbolic significance out of all proportion to its intrinsic value. General Chuikov headed the Soviet resistance among the bombed and shelled ruins of the city, where any technical advantages the Germans had counted for nothing in a primitive struggle in cellars and half-demolished flats and factories among small bodies of men armed with rifles, grenades and knives. While the enemy's attention was firmly focused on the fighting in the ruins and on keeping alive as supplies dwindled, Zhukov saw his chance. At his disposal were a million troops, many of them fresh, and huge numbers of T34 tanks, now being produced by Soviet factories at the rate of 2,000 a year (as opposed to Germany's 500 a year). He realized that if he sent forces through the Romanian and Italian armies to the north-west of Stalingrad and others through Romanian troops to the south-west, then they should be able to meet up and surround the German forces in and around Stalingrad. Zhukov's plan worked.

Operation Blue

General Paulus enters Stalingrad September 1942

Zhukov encircles German forces

The Romanians and Italians, inadequately supplied with anti-tank weapons, fell apart and the Germans found themselves encircled. A relief operation failed and Paulus, ordered by Hitler not to retreat, failed to break out while it might have succeeded. Short of supplies, including food, with his troops interested only in staying alive, Paulus finally defied Hitler by surrendering instead of committing suicide.

Paulus
surrenders
January 1943

THE LIMITS OF THE GERMAN ADVANCE IN RUSSIA, WINTER 1942-3

Altogether 235,000 German and Axis troops were captured during the battle; nearly as many again had been killed. Germany could not easily replace such losses. Despite Goebbels' propaganda about the heroic self-sacrifice of the troops – spoilt by Paulus' shameful surrender – the humiliation of this defeat could hardly be hidden from the German people. The Nazi intelligence agencies reported that many were saying that it represented the beginning of the end. They were right. There was plenty of fight left in the German armies in the east and it took two more years for the Soviets to arrive in Berlin, but Hitler's hopes had been dashed. Japanese aggression had not diverted the British and Americans, who remained determined to destroy Hitler. The despised Soviet Union had weathered the attempt to destroy its armies and industrial potential. By 1943 it was receiving substantial aid from America, chiefly food and means of transportation, but essentially the Soviet Union saved itself. With every month that passed, as the tanks and aircraft poured from the factories, its superiority over the arrogant Germans became more marked. After Stalingrad, if not before, the defeat of the Nazi quest for *Lebensraum* was certain.

4. The Bombing Offensive

The Germans and the Soviets saw bombers primarily as useful adjuncts to the various battlefield weapons. Long-range bombing was a way of attacking the enemy for which the Western powers, Britain and America, showed most enthusiasm. Their leaders, Churchill and Roosevelt, were convinced advocates of this method of attack and they found too that bombing Germany was a means of appeasing Stalin's impatience for Western action against the common enemy. The rationale put forward by the Commander-in-Chief of Bomber Command, Arthur Harris, was that bombing by a large fleet of heavy-bombers was the surest way of destroying the enemy's war potential and hence of knocking him out of the war. The primary targets of the bombing were to be factories, transport facilities, oil depots and the like. In the process a great many civilians were likely to be killed as well, because bombing was extraordinarily inaccurate. A report of 1941 concluded of the British bombing offensive up to that point that only one bomber in three had got within five miles of its target.

Long-range bombing favoured by Allies

Bomber Harris

Despite the manifest limitations of bombing, resources continued to be poured into it during 1942. By the end of the year Britain had two thousand heavy-bombers, including nearly 200 Lancasters, which were to become the mainstay of Bomber Command. The heavy-bombers dropped larger bomb-loads and had a greater range than their lighter predecessors. Carl Spaatz set up the Eighth Air Force in Britain. It was equipped with Boeing B-17s or Flying Fortresses and Churchill usually bombed by day, which allowed much greater accuracy, whereas and the RAF bombed by night. When Churchill and Roosevelt met at Roosevelt in Casablanca at the start of 1943, they agreed to give priority to the Casablanca bombing campaign.

For most of 1943 the results of the war in the air were very mixed. Hitler was always reluctant to invest in defence rather than in offensive weaponry, but even so 70 per cent of German fighter aircraft were kept in the West and took a fearful toll of the streams of bombers sent towards the Reich. There was a constant flow of technical innovations, allowing bombers to find their targets or fighters to detect the bombers, which gave the advantage now to one side, now to the other. 'Window' One of the more important was 'Window': German radar was confused by the dropping of thousands of strips of aluminium foil. When this device was used at Hamburg in a number of raids in July 1943, the loss of bombers was reduced to under 3 per cent, while the combination of high explosive and incendiary bombs overwhelmed the city's emergency services and created a firestorm which destroyed three quarters of the city, killed 40,000 people and made a million Destruction homeless. Yet the destruction of Hamburg did not prove a turning of Hamburg point. The German defences recovered the upper hand and began once more to inflict severe losses on the bombers.

The essential problem for both the British and the American air forces was the strength of the German fighter defence and the inability of their own fighters to escort the bombers beyond the westernmost areas of Germany. The solution was to fit additional, disposable fuel tanks to the Allied fighters. It had been supposed that this change would sacrifice speed and manoeuvrability, but the arrival of the F-51 Mustang proved that this need not be so. This fighter had an American airframe and a Rolls-Royce 'Merlin' engine, and with a range of 1,800 miles it proved the ideal escort fighter. American factories turned it out in huge quantities: in eight months Eighth Air Force quadrupled its fighter strength. From the last months of 1943 the Luftwaffe began to lose fighters more rapidly than they could be replaced, as the escort fighters proved their effectiveness. The loss of experienced pilots became crippling. By the spring of 1944 the Luftwaffe could no longer protect the Reich. The economy was exposed to the bombers. The production of aviation fuel was slowed to the point where the Luftwaffe had to deplete the stocks kept in reserve. Production of explosives was halved as the chemical industry was devastated. The smashing of the railway system starved much of German industry of coal.

The bombing was not pointless, but since the war, the Allies have often been criticized for pursuing a policy which had such horrible effects. Nowhere were the effects more horrible than in Dresden, a city on the Elbe made beautiful by the 18th century Saxon rulers. The city was defenceless, since the anti-aircraft guns had been sent away for use against the Soviets. It was bombed as a significant communications hub in order to assist the Soviet advance. When it was attacked by the British and American bombers on 13th February 1945, a firestorm developed, the results of which were all the worse because the city was crowded with refugees from the east and was inadequately provided with air raid shelters. It is estimated that 35,000 people died. The historic centre was gutted.

Bombing of Dresden

However serious the impact of Allied bombing may have been, the destruction of German air power, which was assisted by bombing, certainly had a significant effect in weakening the German armed forces as they faced the forces of the enemy in 1944-5. The 500 fighters left in the east yielded control of the air to the 13,000 aircraft of the Soviet Union, rendering the ultimate victory of the latter all the

more sure. In the west, the difficult Operation Overlord would hardly
have been possible had the Germans not been compelled to surrender
command of the air because they had only 300 aircraft to pit against
12,000 Allied planes.

Germans lose command of the air

5. Operation Overlord: the Liberation of France, 1944

From the moment that they entered the war at the end of 1941, the
Americans were keen to re-enter the continent of Europe, where
alone, they believed, German power could be given its death blow.
Stalin too kept pressing his allies to open the 'Second Front' in the
hope of relieving German pressure on the USSR. Churchill was
much less keen. He was resolved to prevent the war from turning
into a second Great War, with armies slogging it out in northern
France and young men dying by the hundreds of thousands. He
therefore preferred to weaken Germany by striking at it elsewhere, in
Africa, in Italy, in the Balkans. The Americans feared that it was not
just German forces that were dissipated by these peripheral
campaigns, but also those of the Allies.

It is questionable whether a cheap route to victory existed, any more
than one had in 1914-18. Hitler's Fortress Europe could be defeated
only in a direct confrontation. Nonetheless, men like the American
General Marshall were wildly unrealistic to suppose that Fortress
Europe might be attacked with the slightest prospect of success in
1942 or 1943. Amphibious landings in the face of a well-organized
and resolute enemy are very hard to bring off. Usually, the defender
can rely on fixed defences to do terrible damage to invaders of the
beaches. He can usually reinforce and supply his forces much more
easily than the invader. If invaders attack on a narrow front, they can
be surrounded, but if their front is wide, it is likely to be too thinly
held. The conditions for a successful invasion of France did not exist
before 1944. The Allies had to exercise complete control of the seas
and of the air: they could not have succeeded if U-boats or the

Hazards of amphibious landings

Luftwaffe had been able to interfere. An invasion required a huge effort of industrial production: for example, thousands of landing craft had to be built at a time when many were also required by the war in the Pacific. Huge numbers of men had to be trained: over half a million were landed in France in the first few days of Operation Overlord. Securing British consent to the vast enterprise was not easy. The British had burnt their fingers badly in 1940 and they were terrified that Hitler might force another Dunkirk on them. In the end, the Americans got their way at a conference in Tehran in November 1943, when Churchill was unable to hold out against pressure from Stalin as well as Roosevelt.

Tehran Conference November 1943

Eisenhower was chosen as Supreme Commander of the invasion forces; General Montgomery, popular with the troops and the British public, was to be the British commander. The relationship was to be a difficult one thanks to Monty's prickliness and arrogance. Eisenhower's tact and self-restraint were to be tested to the utmost. But the two were able to agree on the basic plan: to land five divisions on beaches stretching from the mouth of the Seine to the east coast of the Cotentin peninsula; to capture the port of Cherbourg and the town of Caen; and then to break out from the bridgehead and push the German Army out of France.

General Eisenhower

An enormous naval operation was involved. Admiral Ramsay had to arrange for the marshalling and loading with men and supplies of thousands of ships, their assembly at points on the southern shores of England and then their despatch through channels cleared of mines to the Norman coast. Most difficult of all was the task of keeping the supply lines open in unpredictable weather until a port could be captured and made ready. It was decided that this could be done only if the Allies took their harbours with them. Accordingly, two 'Mulberries', as they were code-named, were constructed in sections, towed across the Channel and secured in place. The air forces had a large part to play in preparation for Overlord too. It was essential to prevent the rapid build-up of German forces to throw the invaders

Preparations for Operation Overlord

back into the sea while they were still weak. Intensive bombing of the railway system in France was reckoned to be necessary, though in the event German repair teams were quite successful in limiting the impact on military use of the railways. Much more successful was the destruction of the bridges and tunnels on the routes which connected north-west France with the rest of the country.

The bombing campaign did not remove the need to keep the Germans guessing about the time and place of the invasion as long as possible. Every effort was made to persuade them that the Allies' intention was to attack between Dover and Calais, with a diversionary attack against Norway. German intelligence was persuaded that a First US Army Group (FUSAG) was massing in south-east England: dummy camps, rubber tanks and fake airfields helped to sustain the pretence, which was made yet more convincing by the 'information' the Germans received from double agents. The German 15th Army stayed in the Pas-de-Calais to fight the phantom FUSAG. Despite efforts at camouflage, however, the build-up of troops in south-west England could not fail to attract German notice. Hitler decided that there would be a diversionary landing in Normandy. Though Hitler's new view led to the strengthening of the Norman coastal defences, his belief that the Norman landings were only a side-show prevented a transfer of troops from the Calais area even after the landings had occurred.

FUSAG
decoy

Eisenhower's choice of date for D-Day was 5 June, when the tide and moon would be exactly right. The weather then forced postponement: the seas were too rough and cloud cover denied the Allies the necessary air support. An improvement in the weather was forecast for the next day and, taking a chance, Eisenhower gave the order to proceed. The poor weather immediately before D-Day led the Germans to conclude that an invasion was not imminent. Rommel, in charge of the defending forces, had even gone home to celebrate his wife's birthday. On the three easternmost beaches where the Commonwealth troops came ashore, German resistance, stunned by

D-Day
landings
June 6th
1944

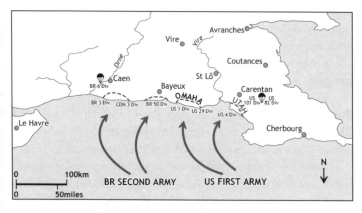

THE NORMANDY LANDINGS, JUNE 1944

the bombardment from the sea and from the air, was rapidly overcome. At Utah beach the Americans had an even easier time. Only at Omaha, the beach in between the British ones and Utah, did things go seriously wrong. Because of the cloud, the aerial bombardment had missed the shore defences altogether, and the naval bombardment had also been inaccurate. This happened also to be the area where German defences were strongest. Yet the Americans did eventually get through the German defences, though at terrible cost in lives.

Rommel had failed to mount strong assaults on the Allies while they were still on the beaches. Many of the reinforcements had been kept too far back and Allied air attacks and the French Resistance were doing their best to impede the movement of German forces. Those which got through arrived piecemeal and could not deliver an adequate punch. The German aim in the next phase of the campaign was to hold a line about ten miles from the coast and prevent the Allies from taking their objectives, the port of Cherbourg to the west and the town of Caen to the east. Allied progress was very slow, partly because the Germans had orders not to give ground, partly because the countryside was the *bocage*, a land of narrow lanes between high banks topped with thick hedges. The landscape made defence much

Rearguard action by the French Resistance

121

easier and deprived Allied tanks of all mobility. The Allied task was made harder yet by the gales in the Channel on and after June 19th, which reduced their supplies to a trickle. The sole achievement of the

Allies capture Cherbourg

last days of June was the capture of Cherbourg, which provided the Allies with a permanent port, once it had been put in order. But the Americans at the base of the Cotentin peninsula and Montgomery around Caen made little progress. Eisenhower was dismayed as a stalemate similar to that of 1914-18 seemed to loom.

Eisenhower thought that the way to prevent a stalemate was to launch a vigorous offensive all along the front. He was at loggerheads with Montgomery, who considered that the enemy had to be induced to concentrate his effort at a single point, which would render easy a breakthrough elsewhere. Bringing up over 600 tanks, the Germans focused on the Caen area, which they saw as the gateway to the Seine Valley and Paris. Monty's strategy was to tie up and wear them down near Caen, while Bradley, in charge of the American sector, broke through in the west, where the Germans had under 200 tanks. Unfortunately, Bradley was delayed first by lack of supplies, then by the weather, but finally on 25 July he went on to the offensive, aided by devastating air bombardments unleashed on the Germans and by tanks modified by the addition of eight steel teeth, which could cut through the hedgerows and thereby enable the tanks to drive rapidly across country. The Germans had received few reinforcements and inadequate supplies and when the 15th Army began to arrive from the Calais area it was piecemeal, so disrupted were communications. The German forces were hampered further by Hitler, who insisted that they should not retreat and later that they should launch impossible counter-attacks. There could therefore be no fighting withdrawal in good order, as in 1918, or any stand behind a readily defensible line further east.

German positions in France collapse

In August the entire German position in France collapsed. A plan for an Allied landing in southern France was activated, and everywhere the French began to take a part in their own liberation.

On 26 August General de Gaulle, leader of the Free French forces, which had fought alongside the British and Americans, entered Paris in triumph. By early September the British had reached Antwerp in Belgium. For the Germans the three-month campaign had been a disaster. Around 250,000 were dead or wounded, 200,000 were prisoners and almost all their equipment was lost. Though many individuals struggled back to Germany, the German army in France had ceased to exist. For the Allies, too, the campaign had been a very bloody one. The contrast between huge Soviet losses in the East and relatively light Allied losses in the West is often made. This contrast reflects the length of the eastern campaigns and the terrible treatment of Soviet prisoners of war. The fighting in France was brief, but very intense. The British army group of Canadians, Poles and British lost over 80,000, the Americans suffered heavier losses still – more than 120,000 in a mere three months.

Liberation of Paris August 1944

Heavy losses during the Allied campaign

6. The Collapse of Nazi Germany, 1945

Towards the end of 1944 both the Soviet forces assailing Germany in the east and the Allied forces in the west experienced supply problems because of their recent rapid advances. Hitler took advantage of the respite to attempt a breakout in the west in December 1944. Two hundred thousand German troops, spearheaded by 600 tanks, were to break through the American lines in the Ardennes and, in a manoeuvre similar to that proposed by Manstein in 1940, were to head for the sea, cutting off and encircling all the armies to the north. This time round, however, the Germans were far weaker than they had been in 1940. They wholly lacked superiority in the air and were bombarded relentlessly whenever the weather was good enough. Even more disastrously, their supplies of petrol were inadequate. Nor were the Americans such feeble fighters as Hitler maintained. The Battle of the Bulge, named after the salient into the Allied front which it created, was another German failure. Losses on both sides were

The Battle of the Bulge December 1944

roughly equal, but the Americans could replace both tanks and men. The Germans could not.

Hitler's hopes were now based mainly on the 'wonder-weapons' which Germany was developing. A campaign of bombing from aeroplanes in early 1944 had not proved especially successful, but by June 1944 the V-1, a pilotless flying bomb, had been developed. The 'V' stood for *Vergeltung* or 'retribution', which indicated the prime purpose of the bombs as the exacting of revenge for the Allies' bombing campaign. The 'doodle-bugs' had some psychological effect on the population of south-east England, but its inaccuracy, vulnerability to anti-aircraft fire and fighter attack and the overrunning of its launch sites in 1944 meant that it was not a war-winning weapon. Work had also proceeded on the V-2, a rocket powered by liquid fuel, which was the brain-child of scientist Wernher von Braun. The weapon encountered innumerable teething problems, but some rockets were finally fired at London in September 1944. Defence against them was virtually impossible, given their speed, but they could carry no more than a ton of high explosive. Far more were fired at liberated Belgium than at Britain. The total death toll is thought to have been about 5,000, far lower than the death toll among the slave labourers forced to work on the weapon. The Nazi regime encouraged work on other weapons: nerve gas and the atomic bomb, for example. Yet it lacked the time or the large economic resources that their full development required. These weapons became another delusive hope with which Hitler tried to bolster the German people's faltering confidence in his regime.

The V-1 'doodlebug'

Wernher von Braun

VII

THE WAR AGAINST JAPAN IN THE PACIFIC

1. Japanese Ambitions and Policies

EVER since its modernization in the later 19th century, Japan had sought to enhance its international status and to acquire a colonial empire, which seemed an essential trapping of greatness. The country enjoyed some success in this respect. Wars with China and Russia in the late 19th and early 20th century had made Japan the dominant power in East Asia and brought it control of Korea, Formosa (Taiwan) and the southern half of Sakhalin. It possessed too important rights in Manchuria, especially control over a 700-mile stretch of railway.

The most important issue in east Asia concerned the future of the huge state of China. After the end of the Empire in 1911, the country had dissolved into the fiefdoms of competing warlords, but after the First World War, there were signs of an emergent Chinese nationalism, *Kuomintang* reflected in the rise of a Nationalist Party, the *Kuomintang* (KMT). The Western powers, including America, upheld China's independence and integrity and favoured the KMT, the head of which, after 1924, was Chiang Kai-shek. Japan accepted the same policy as the West in the 1920s, but the onset of the Great Depression strengthened forces in Japan which called for greater economic self-sufficiency. For Japan, a country with limited resources, economic self-sufficiency could be achieved only by expansion. The obvious direction for expansion was the still weak state of China. In 1931 the Japanese Kwantung Army, which safeguarded Japanese possessions in Manchuria, took an expansionist initiative by staging a clash with the Chinese on the railway and then proceeding to establish a puppet state Manchukuo called Manchukuo, nominally ruled by the deposed last Emperor of China. Despite China's appeal to the League of Nations, no power

Japanese Empire from 1870
Acquired by 1932
Acquired by 1937
Acquired by 1938
Acquired by 1939
Acquired by 1940
Acquired by 1942

SOVIET UNION

Sea of
Okhotsk

Kuril Is
(1875)

Southern
Sakhalin
(1905)

MANCHURIA
(1905-1932 Puppet State)

Harbin

Vladivostok

Hokkaido

INNER
MONGOLIA

JEHOL
1932

KOREA
(1905 Protectorate,
1910 annexed)

Sea of
Japan

JAPAN

Tokyo

Peking

Seoul

SHANSI

Shantung Pen
(1915-1917)

Tsushima

Shikoku

KIANGSO

Yellow
Sea

Strait

CHINA

Hankow
(1937)

Ningpo

INDIA
(Br.)

Nanchang

Ryukyu Is
(1872-1879)

Daito Island
(1876)

Amoy

East China Sea

BURMA
(Br.)

TONGKING

Hanoi

Macao

Hong Kong

TAIWAN
(1895)

PACIFIC

Rangoon
(1942)

Canton
(1937)

(1941)

THAILAND
(1941)

FRENCH
INDO-
CHINA

Hainan
(1939)

Luzon

Philippine Sea

OCEAN

Andaman
Sea

Saigon

South China Sea

Manila

PHILIPPINES
(1942)

Yap (1914)

Gulf of
Thailand

Leyte

Sulu Sea

MALAYA
(Br.)

Natuna
Besar

Brunei

BR.
NORTH
BORNEO

Mindanao

Palau (1914)

Strait of Malacca

SINGAPORE
(1942)

BR. BRUNEI

Celebes Sea

0

800km

Sumatra
(Dutch)

BR. SARAWAK

Borneo

0

500miles

The Expansion of Japanese-Ruled Territory, 1870-1942

Japan leaves
League of
Nations
1933

went beyond verbal condemnation of Japan. Nonetheless, Japan was now diplomatically isolated, as its exit from the League of Nations in 1933 underlined.

Government propaganda had no difficulty in arousing Japanese popular support for its policies. In view of the existence of Western colonial empires, Western attitudes of disapproval of Japanese policies in China could easily be represented as hypocritical. Anti-Western attitudes gained ground as the government spoke of 'national renovation' and emphasized traditional culture and mythology. Hirohito had ascended the imperial throne in 1926 and his reign was portrayed as the inauguration of a new age which would renew and extend the triumphs of the reign of his grandfather, the Emperor Meiji, when Japan had won its war with Russia. The Emperor was portrayed as a living god, the symbol of the Japanese nation. His divinity did not mean that the Emperor was the main influence on policy-making. Great importance was attached to the emergence of a consensus among the leading figures, who included the heads of the army and navy. Despite differences over tactics, these men agreed that Japan, as a nation with a superior culture, was destined to dominate the surrounding peoples. The middle ranks of the military, in particular, became imbued with an aggressive and arrogant militarism.

Emperor Hirohito

In July 1937 near the Marco Polo Bridge south of Beijing Chinese troops fired on Japanese soldiers and the Japanese government took the decision to expand the incident into full-scale war. The war that followed was notable for Japanese atrocities which shocked the world. When Chiang Kai-shek's capital Nanjing (Nanking) fell in December 1937, 200,000 Chinese civilians and prisoners of war were murdered in six weeks and countless women were raped. Western opinion became intensely anti-Japanese and sympathy with China grew. The greatest problem for the Japanese was their inability to end the war. Chiang had withdrawn to Chongqing in the deep interior, from where he could keep resistance going, with help from the USSR, the USA and Britain and France. The Japanese invited the Chinese to participate in creating 'a new order for stability in East Asia' and some were tempted, but Chiang rightly calculated that few Chinese nationalists would be ready to become Japan's junior partners, especially given the continued brutality of Japanese rule in large areas of China. By this time, 600,000 Japanese troops were tied down in China and there was no prospect of Japan's ever being able to remove them. Moreover, Japan had by no means achieved the economic self-sufficiency that it needed. In

Marco-Polo Bridge

The 'Rape' of Nanking

particular, it still depended on the United States for its oil and its metal. Yet the invasion of China inevitably harmed relations with the USA. The invasion of China, originally presented as an easy way for Japan to secure its interests, had turned out to be a very dangerous gamble.

The dangers of Japan's position became clear in 1939. The USA was increasingly hostile. Britain, France and the Netherlands were worried as the Japanese extended their control southwards to various islands belonging to China. Most serious of all was a series of clashes with Soviet troops to the north-west of Manchukuo. The Red Army showed clearly that it was a much more formidable adversary than the Tsarist army had been. Perhaps Hitler should have taken more notice.

Japanese isolation
The obvious way out of isolation was for Japan to convert the Anti-Comintern Pact, which it had signed with Hitler, into a full alliance. Yet it was far from clear how Hitler and Mussolini could be of any help to Japan in resolving its problems. In any case, in August 1939 Hitler allied with one of Japan's most formidable enemies, the USSR.

The course of the war in Western Europe in 1940 appeared to change Japan's situation. The threat from Germany forced Britain and France to suspend aid for Chiang Kai-shek flowing through Hong Kong, Burma and French Indo-China. Then the defeat of France and the Netherlands and the precarious situation of Britain seemed to offer what the Army Minister called a 'golden opportunity' to expand to the south at the expense of the European colonial empires. The key prize was the Dutch East Indies and their oil. If the Japanese did turn southwards, then they would have to end their conflict with the USSR. A Neutrality Pact was to be signed between

Soviet-Japanese Neutrality Pact
Japan and the USSR in April 1941. A much greater problem was the possibility that southwards expansion might bring on a conflict with the USA. Some of the naval leaders did not believe that Japan could win such a conflict.

It seemed to some of the Japanese leaders that there might be a way of preventing a war with the USA over expansion to the south. It was to make a firm alliance with Germany and Italy. This alliance, the Tripartite Pact, would, it was argued, act as a deterrent to the USA and inhibit it from continuing to aid Chiang Kai-shek and from upholding the existing balance of power in the Far East. Many in Japan felt a certain kinship with Italy and Germany, seeing them as fellow 'have-not' powers rising up against the existing order arranged by the 'have' powers for their profit. In September 1940 Japan signed the Tripartite Pact. Tripartite Pact September 1940

Japan had miscalculated. Its alliance with Hitler's Germany merely confirmed all America's suspicions that Japan was an Asian equivalent of Nazi Germany whose aggressions would have to be stopped. Roosevelt was not yet ready for open war, but Chiang Kai-shek was given $100 million, which made a solution to Japan's problem of China even less likely, and the USA imposed an embargo on the export of iron and scrap metal to Japan. This was an important sanction, which indicated that a crippling embargo on oil could follow at any time. Japan had brought war with the USA and Britain a great deal closer, while still uncertain whether it had a chance of winning.

2. Lightning War in the Pacific, 1941-2

In September 1940 the Japanese occupied northern Indo-China by agreement with Vichy France. In July 1941 Japan extended its control over the whole of Indo-China. The Americans had broken one of the important Japanese codes and the information gleaned confirmed American suspicions that Japan was preparing to attack Malaya and the Dutch East Indies, no doubt with a view to including them in the Japanese economic system. Japan stood to gain rubber, tin and oil. America would be denied access to those important raw materials. Roosevelt at once took steps against Japan. All Japanese assets in USA were frozen, effectively closing down trade between the two countries. The Dutch government, operating in exile from London, and the British government followed suit. These actions threatened to undermine the Japanese economy and armed forces by depriving Japan occupies French Indo-China September 1940 Japanese assets in USA frozen July 1941

THE ATTACK ON PEARL HARBOR, 7 DECEMBER 1941
Courtesy of the Imperial War Museum

them of crucial commodities such as oil. The Japanese government had therefore to make in the near future an irrevocable decision. It could decide to make peace with the USA. Proposals for a summit meeting with President Roosevelt were put forward, but peace was available only if the Japanese made large concessions on China. Too much effort had been invested in China and too many Japanese lives had been lost there for Japan to be able to regard as honourable concessions that were large enough to satisfy the Americans and the Chinese Nationalists whom they patronized. The peace overtures therefore led nowhere and the Japanese felt that they had no alternative but to go to war. Many of them went with a heavy heart. Admiral Yamamoto had said in 1940, 'It's out of the question! To fight the United States is like fighting the whole world. But it has been decided. So I will fight my best.'

Yamamoto was the planner of the attack with which the war began, the destruction of the American Pacific fleet at Pearl Harbor. The Japanese believed that the elimination of their fleet might impel the Americans to make peace, but even if it did not, it would at least render them impotent to interfere as the Japanese established their Greater East Asian Co-Prosperity Sphere. Accordingly, the Japanese prepared a force of six aircraft carriers with over 350 aircraft, the majority of them bombers, escorted by a powerful fleet of capital ships. They set sail from the Kurile Islands on a route which avoided shipping lanes and where detection by American reconnaissance aircraft was unlikely. When the Japanese struck at Pearl Harbor at 7.55 on a Sunday morning, 7 December1941, they achieved complete surprise. Four battleships and seven other naval vessels were sunk and more, including four battleships, were severely damaged. American airpower was harmed too: large numbers of aircraft were destroyed or damaged. In all, 3,435 American servicemen were killed, whereas Japanese losses were under a hundred.

Destruction of American fleet at Pearl Harbor December 1941

The Japanese achieved one of their key aims, in that they had knocked out the only force in the area capable of seriously interfering with their plans of conquest. On the other hand, in many ways the results of their raid on Pearl Harbor were disappointing. Not a single American aircraft carrier had been in port and yet it was on the carriers, not on elderly battleships, that American power in the Pacific chiefly depended. As it turned out, not even the battleships had been disposed of for good. All but one were afterwards repaired and restored for war service. The Japanese bombers had also lacked the right sort of weaponry to destroy the American dockyard facilities or even their fuel tanks. Pearl Harbor continued to be a very useful base for American operations in the Pacific. It was only in the short term that American offensive power was damaged. Above all, the Japanese had seriously miscalculated the effect of their actions on American opinion. Far from inclining them to make concessions to the Japanese, the attack, which had been launched with no warning and without

America
declares war
on Japan

even a declaration of war, united Americans as nothing else could have done. In Congress only one vote was cast against the declaration of war on Japan. The Japanese had aroused the implacable wrath of an enemy vastly more powerful than they were.

British
garrison in
Hong Kong
surrenders

At first, American wrath did not seem to matter. The Japanese carried all before them in South-East Asia. The American-dominated Philippines were attacked immediately after Pearl Harbor. The islands were within range of the Japanese air bases on Formosa and the armed forces under General MacArthur were too few to have much hope of successfully resisting Japanese invasion. The British outposts in the Far East came under attack too. Hong Kong was indefensible. The air bases on Formosa were only 400 miles away and the Japanese controlled the Chinese mainland. There was no way of keeping open the sea lanes to the colony. It was unfortunate that the garrison had not been withdrawn, for the inevitable surrender at Christmas 1941 meant that 12,000 men passed into captivity.

Japan attacks
British in
Malaya

Meanwhile, the British had also come under attack in Malaya. Japanese troops were ferried from occupied Indo-China across the Gulf of Thailand to northern Malaya; others came overland through Thailand. The British were woefully unprepared. They had no tanks and were much inferior to the Japanese in aircraft. In troops the British-led forces outnumbered the Japanese, but they were poorly equipped and trained. The best hope of the British was to interfere with the Japanese landings, by using their naval forces. Realising that the decision to cut off imports crucial to Japan might provoke the country to war, Churchill had sent to the Far East what he fondly hoped might be a deterrent force. His plan had been to send a new battleship, HMS *Prince of Wales*, accompanied by a battle-cruiser and an aircraft-carrier, but in the end no carrier was sent. The omission was to prove fatal. The naval force did not deter the Japanese, but it did take part in the war by moving to intercept the Japanese landing craft on the Malayan coast. But by 1941, the big ships no longer ruled the waves. The Japanese called up their air power and sank both British capital ships. Churchill later wrote of his reaction to the disaster thus: 'In all the war I never received a more direct shock.' He belonged to a generation that thought of battleships as the solid foundations of British power and their vulnerability in an age of air power had now been cruelly exposed.

The naval disaster doomed Malaya. The British-led troops were repeatedly outflanked by Japanese manoeuvres through supposedly impenetrable jungle. The British never succeeded in concentrating their forces, which were defeated again and again. Constant harassment from the air was demoralizing. By the end of January 1942 the mainland was lost and the Japanese were plainly about to attack Singapore. The city had been turned into an impregnable fortress in the inter-war years, when it became the strong-point of the British Empire in the Far East. The Japanese needed to take it if they were to dominate the Pacific and they also wished to cut off an important source of aid for the Chinese Nationalists, who had wealthy supporters in the Chinese community of Singapore. The defences of Singapore had been designed against an invasion from the sea, but the Japanese attacked from the Malay peninsula, across the narrow channels which divided the islands of Singapore from the mainland. The great guns were capable of being turned in that direction, but they fired armour-piercing shells rather than the high explosive shells that would have been more useful against the Japanese coming across in any boats they could find. The British commanders spread their troops thinly round the coast and the various sea inlets made it hard for the different units to give support to each other. Consequently, the superior numbers of defending troops failed against the numerically inferior attackers. The lack of adequate air cover was also demoralising. As the situation worsened, Churchill gave orders that 'commanders and senior officers should die with their troops', since, he said, 'the honour of the British Empire and the British army is at stake'. The commanders of the defenders lacked Churchill's almost Japanese enthusiasm for self-sacrifice. With supplies of food and

Japanese attack Singapore February 1942

water running low and civilian casualties mounting, by 15 February General Percival saw no point in continuing to sustain a resistance which seemed hopeless and he determined to surrender. He and his 80,000 troops were taken prisoner. There was no precedent for surrender on this scale in the whole of British military history. Churchill felt the disgrace keenly. It was, he said, the 'worst disaster' in British history. It is doubtful if many of his compatriots agreed with him. Though the German menace was close and immediate, the Japanese threat was remote.

Singapore surrenders

To other parts of the Empire, however, the Japanese threat had come to appear very real. As early as December 1941 the Japanese began their onslaught on Burma, one of the western gateways to China, which the Japanese determined to seal. Rangoon had to be evacuated in March 1942 and British forces were chased out of the rest of the country by May. The army was saved, but the Burma Road to China was cut. At the fall of Singapore, some Indian soldiers were among those who surrendered. Some were willing to join an Indian national army, set up by Japan, which claimed to favour Indian national liberty. This Army eventually had perhaps as many as 42,000 members and there were fears that it might win many more recruits and weaken British India. The Japanese Navy was able to penetrate the Indian Ocean and the British became anxious for the security of Ceylon (Sri Lanka). If the island fell to the Japanese, British communications with India and Australia would be endangered. In addition, since the fall of Malaya, Ceylon had become an important source of rubber. The military and naval forces on the island were accordingly built up. It was probably the arrival of these reinforcements which prompted the Japanese air raids on Colombo in April 1942. The Japanese lacked the manpower to extend their empire yet further. They were thinly stretched already and the army vetoed the tentative plans of the navy to invade Ceylon. Yet the Japanese wanted to deter their enemies from further interference in the lands to the east of the Indian Ocean and in this

Rangoon evacuated March 1942

Burma Road to China cut off

they succeeded. The British naval forces retired to Bombay (Mumbai) and East Africa.

The Japanese had also expanded their control towards the south. The Dutch government in exile had declared war on them after Pearl Harbor and the Japanese soon responded by establishing air superiority over the East Indies and landing on many of the islands. Their main aim was to exploit the resources of the area, especially its oil. After two months or so, most resistance ceased. Thereafter, Japan's main concern was to safeguard what it had gained. Australia it sought to cow by raids on northern ports such as Darwin and Broome. Panicking Australians thought that it might be necessary to evacuate the whole of the country north of Brisbane. The Japanese army, however, showed no inclination to release the huge number of troops that would have been necessary to conquer the country. A more practical plan was to capture New Guinea, and then to thrust through the Solomon Islands towards Fiji and Samoa. Australia was dangerous to Japan only as a springboard for American power; if isolated from America, it would effectively be neutralized. Checks to the Japanese advance were administered as early as the spring of 1942, when American naval power forced the Japanese to abandon plans for an amphibious attack on the south coast of Papua New Guinea. Later in the year, the Australians, with American aid, stopped an overland attack with the same objective after fierce fighting in the jungles of the island's interior.

Japanese air raids on Australian ports

3. The Prisoners of the Japanese

The tidal wave of Japanese conquest in the last month of 1941 and the first few months of 1942 brought into their hands very large numbers of prisoners of war and large numbers of Western civilians who had been living in the places which the Japanese overran. Little was known about Japanese treatment of these people while the war was on, but since it ended, the Japanese treatment of those who fell into their hands has become notorious.

Japanese Prisoners of War

The statistics are suggestive. Of British and American prisoners of war in German hands, just 4 per cent died, but of the 132,000 Allied POWs in Japanese hands, 27 per cent perished. The chances of survival of the 130,000 internees in the Dutch East Indies were not markedly different: 30,000 died. Asians were not spared by Japanese taskmasters. A quarter of the Chinese labourers sent to Japan died and around a fifth of the Javanese, Burmese, Indians and Chinese who worked on the Burma-Thailand Railway.

Death toll on the Burma-Thailand Railway

The Western and Indian prisoners had been conditioned to regard surrender and subsequent captivity as a misfortune which might, through no fault of their own, befall any fighting men. The captured soldier had therefore a right to decent treatment. The Japanese saw things differently. A fighting man who surrendered had lost his honour and forfeited his dignity as a human being. He retained no rights and could be treated as a slave, bound to perform whatever tasks his captors imposed upon him. The task imposed on many of the POWs was the building of a railway to connect Thailand and Burma, a major engineering challenge, since the line had to go over mountains and through thick jungle. The project was to be accomplished largely with human labour and hand-tools. Cuttings and embankments were made without the aid of any earth-moving equipment; 24-foot lengths of steel rail were manoeuvred into position by human strength alone. Food was often short, even for the Japanese supervisors, especially as the track got further from the railhead, and it was virtually impossible to avoid contracting malaria and various fevers.

Some prisoners were sent to labour in Japan. Transportation there exposed the prisoners to the danger of attack by US submarines, which the Japanese did not seek to reduce by identifying the ships which carried POWs. It is reckoned that at least 10,000 prisoners perished at sea. Chances of survival were reduced by the reluctance of the Japanese captains of passing ships to pick up any but Japanese survivors. Arrangements for providing the prisoners on board the ships with food and drink were often almost non-existent. On the voyage of the *Oryoku Maru* in 1944 water and tea were periodically lowered in kegs and only those nearest the ladders got a drink. When prisoners arrived in Japan, they often found that working and living conditions were bad. For the prisoners doing 12-hour shifts at the Omuta chemical works, life consisted of no more than work and sleep. The slave labourers were not looked after. Unheated barrack-style accommodation could be desperately cold at night. Often, nothing was done to treat the illnesses, often deficiency diseases, from which the labourers suffered.

Conditions in the various Japanese camps were far from uniform, but complaints about inadequate food were very general. The prisoners in Rangoon, or Changi, Singapore, who were permitted gardens in which they grew green vegetables, were unusually fortunate. Most prisoners had to subsist on bowls of rice and thin soup, a diet lacking in essential nutrients and quite inadequate for those required to do heavy labour. Allied POWs were entitled to receive International Red Cross parcels, but their issue to the prisoners depended on the whims of local commanders and often the prison staff pillaged the contents. Families dispatched huge numbers of parcels for imprisoned relatives, but these too often failed to reach the intended recipients.

Conditions in Japanese camps

In some places internees formed a community which was allowed to run many of its own affairs. In Changi Camp in Singapore perhaps the biggest enemy for the inmates, cut off from the wider world and unable to travel, was boredom. To combat the tedium the camp acquired the contents of Singapore Library, which made possible the establishment of what the internees called Changi University. POWs and many internees, however, were directly subject to Japanese officials who wielded arbitrary authority in a cruel and capricious manner. Offences such as building a radio receiver could be punished by long periods of standing to attention in the tropical sun and by savage beatings which might break limbs and crack ribs. Arbitrary bayonetings and beheadings were not unknown. The Ministry of War had issued regulations stating that prisoners were to be treated in accordance with the Geneva Convention, but it is clear that the military took no notice and that no one tried to make them do so.

Contra-
ventions of
the Geneva
Convention

It is possible to suggest some excuses for the Japanese failure to treat their prisoners humanely. In the early stages of the Pacific War, there were simply too many prisoners and the Japanese were unready to look after them properly. Medical supplies and sometimes food too were always short in the Japanese Empire. Every army has its quota of sadists. Yet the decision to expend the lives of thousands on the Thailand-Burma railway or the indifference to Allied prisoners adrift on the sea can be explained only by reference to the military ethos and scale of values which was dominant in Japan. The soldiers looked down even on civilians of their own society. Lower still in their scale of values were the civilians of other races, whether of European or Asian origin. Utterly contemptible were soldiers who by surrender had sacrificed their honour to preserve their lives. This ethos had no room for compassion for the powerless and unfortunate. It was associated with the fighting spirit which made possible Japan's successes, but it also implied the racial arrogance which doomed Japan's Greater East Asian Co-Prosperity Sphere even before it was founded by alienating the Chinese, Filipinos, Indonesians and others, without whose co-operation it could not endure.

4. British Recovery: the Campaigns in Burma, 1944-5

The early months of the Pacific War were utterly ignominious for Britain. The Prime Minister felt the humiliation keenly and thought it essential for Britain to take action to restore its battered reputation in the region. Yet inevitably Britain had to concentrate on the European and Atlantic theatres of war, since there the very survival of Britain was at stake. There were few resources left over to devote to the war against Japan, which was mostly about Britain's reputation.

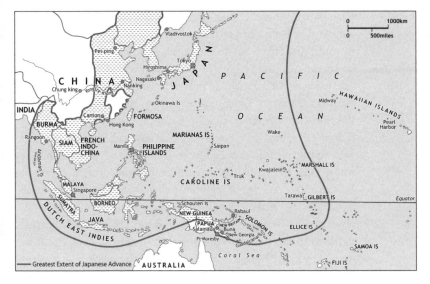

THE WAR IN ASIA: The Far East Front

In the Pacific, even more than in Europe and the Atlantic, the United States would have to take the lead and Britain would have to fit in with its plans. It was agreed that the USA would deal with Japan in the Pacific Ocean, while Britain took over the anti-Japanese effort in the Indian Ocean. Churchill liked the idea of an amphibious assault on Sumatra, which might have led on to the recovery of Singapore, an obsession with the Prime Minister. His military advisors were against the scheme, but in any case the USA would have had to provide the shipping and it was unwilling to do so. It preferred an attack on the Japanese in northern Burma.

American support of the Kuomintang

The Americans believed that the Chinese Army under Chiang Kai-shek, which they were trying to build up into a serious military force, could play a large part in the liberation of eastern Asia from Japanese domination. It needed to be supplied and to that end the Americans aimed to open the Burma Road, a tenuous link between India and

China which wound through the mountains and jungles of northern Burma. The British had no faith whatever in the ability of the Chinese to contribute effectively to the defeat of Japan. No doubt, British scepticism was based largely on racial prejudice – Churchill famously referred to the Chinese as '425 million pigtails' – but their doubts about the military value of Chiang's army were to be justified. Nonetheless, the British co-operated with the Americans, since no other way of restoring their prestige in South-East Asia was available. The Americans were equally unenthusiastic about co-operating with the British. They realized that Churchill hoped to restore the British Empire in the Far East and suspected that he might even attempt to expand it by annexing Thailand. They had no intention of assisting Churchill to achieve these objectives. Yet British co-operation in India and Burma could be useful to them. In the East the Anglo-American alliance held, but it was marred by mutual suspicion and, at times, antagonism.

In the spring of 1942, the Japanese had succeeded in conquering Burma at the cost of only 2,000 Japanese lives. Before the Second World War ended, however, another 104,000 lives were to be lost holding on to what Japan had so easily gained. For a long time the British mounted no effective counter-attack. In 1943 the British public was fascinated by the exploits of Orde Wingate's 'Chindits', named after a winged mythical beast depicted in Burmese temples. They operated in the jungle behind Japanese lines and were dependent on air-borne supplies. They tied down Japanese troops, but their achievements were hardly proportionate to their heavy losses. In the end, it was the Japanese who reactivated the Burmese front by launching an operation to seize Imphal and Kohima in northeast India. The operation was designed to prevent a planned British advance into Burma and, if possible, to trigger a popular revolt against British domination by giving the Indian National Army a prominent role. The Japanese plan was absurdly ambitious, given the difficulties of supply, almost entirely dependent on slow-moving bullocks. They were unable to deploy tanks or artillery. As earlier in

Cost to Japan of holding Burma

Japan threatens British India

140

the war, they achieved surprise and moved rapidly to cut off British strongholds, but the British were now able to supply threatened points by air, so that Japanese surprise and speed were no longer decisive. British control of the air also enabled them to attack the Japanese supply line, which meant that the Japanese troops began to starve. One of the most significant British assets was the generalship of William Slim, a calm leader whose concern for his men won their total loyalty. The breaking of the monsoon in July 1944, while the Japanese were still trying to hold on round Imphal, completed the discomfiture of the invading army. The campaign had been utterly disastrous. Over a third of the Japanese fighting men of the army were dead. The Indian National Army had collapsed. Huge numbers of indispensable pack animals had perished. The Japanese were to reinforce their ground troops before the next spring, but their fighting power on the Burmese front had been permanently crippled. Some of the weaknesses of the Japanese approach to war had been starkly revealed: the preference for attack, which had led to the campaign; the belief that fighting spirit could overcome every disadvantage; and the preference for death in a hopeless situation over retreat and withdrawal.

Leadership 'Bill' Slim

The Burmese campaigns of 1944-5 turned out to be the swansong of the British Imperial army. Under Slim served not only British soldiers, but also Gurkhas, East and West Africans and Indians from many parts of the sub-continent. The war was very different from the war simultaneously being fought in Europe. It was less mechanized: the soldiers had to be accompanied by a variety of pack animals, such as bullocks dyed green (for camouflage), mules and elephants, the last particularly valued for their bridge-building skills. Formal infantry attacks supported by artillery were replaced by infiltration and encirclement of enemy positions, which required skilful infantry and able junior officers. One reason for the early Japanese successes had been their enemies' inability to cope with jungle fighting. The Japanese never thought that the British were adept at fighting in the

Techniques of jungle warfare

jungle: they were too noisy, disliked close combat and were unready to fight to the death. Yet certainly the British and their Indian and African allies had greatly improved since 1941-2. For both sides the Burmese jungles remained very unpleasant places to fight. More casualties were due to disease than to enemy action. Skin diseases, dysentery, malaria and typhus all took a heavy toll. The insects and the heat, dampness and dirt made the lives of the troops exceptionally uncomfortable. The campaigns in Burma were not entirely an imperial affair. Unlike in 1941-2, Slim's army had American air support. The transport aircraft were indispensable and the bombing of bridges, Japanese positions and later of railyards was useful. The Japanese air force had almost disappeared from the sky at this stage of the war.

During the winter of 1944-5 Slim's army crossed the River Chindwin and finally opened the road to China. They at last left behind the claustrophobic jungle and came out on to the central plain of Burma, a land of paddy fields and villages. The spine of the country is

Allied army crosses Irawaddy River

the mighty Irrawaddy River. The newly appointed Japanese general Kimura was confident that Slim would cross it north of Mandalay. Slim planned feints in that direction in order to get Kimura to commit his forces to the north while the bulk of the British forces drove on southwards, achieved the difficult feat of crossing the river in a makeshift fleet of inadequate boats and took control of the road and rail network. Slim's plans worked well. He was greatly assisted by the Japanese lack of planes to carry out reconnaissance from the air, which would have revealed where his armies were, and he was aided too by the enemy's lack of rapid transport, which made it difficult to switch troops from one place to another. Central Burma was an area where the British could make full use of their aircraft and artillery and where the Japanese lack of anti-tank weapons told heavily against them. After Slim had outmanoeuvred the Japanese and slipped past them to the south, they were forced to attack his forces, which meant exposing themselves to British offensive weapons. Underfed and under-equipped, the Japanese could do little beyond showing that they knew how to die. Their own earlier merciless conduct rebounded against them in that it was impossible for British officers to restrain the blood lust of their men as Japanese units broke up. The Burma campaign proceeded swiftly to its conclusion. On 3 May 1945 the Japanese abandoned Rangoon.

The exploits of Bill Slim and his army were little appreciated by those in charge of the British war effort. Immediately after his triumphal entry into Rangoon, Slim was relieved of his command by his immediate superior. He was soon reinstated, but never received due recognition from Sir Alan Brooke or Churchill. It was not that they had a personal animus against the general, but rather that they never attached much importance to the Burma Campaign. Their view reflected opinion in Britain, where Slim's army was what it sometimes ruefully called itself, 'the forgotten army'. Yet the campaign fought in Burma in 1944-5 has a claim to be considered the most brilliant and successful British (as opposed to Anglo-American) campaign of the Second World War. The Japanese had lost a large territory and 100,000 soldiers. British and Indian losses had been relatively light, at one for every thirteen Japanese. The slowness of progress in 1944 led many to underestimate Slim's achievement, but the nature of the terrain prevented a rapid advance and in any case Slim made up for it by the speed of his victory in 1945. The Burma Campaign brought the curtain down on two centuries of British colonial wars in Asia in a worthy manner. Yet it is undoubtedly true that the Burma campaign contributed little to Japan's ultimate defeat, which was brought about by American action in the Pacific.

5. American Victories over Japan, 1942-5

After their success at Pearl Harbor and their subsequent conquest of South-East Asia, the Japanese sought to enhance the security of their Co-Prosperity Sphere by eliminating what remained of American naval power in the South Pacific and seizing the island of Midway.

Midway was the westernmost point of the Hawaiian archipelago and an American base. The Japanese hoped to transform it into a base of their own, from which Hawaii could be threatened.

The confrontation over Midway occurred in the early summer of 1942, when the Americans had not yet rebuilt their naval power after Pearl Harbor. To pit against the massive forces of Yamamoto, who had four aircraft carriers and seven battleships, the American Admiral Nimitz disposed of three carriers. They were under strength in fighters to protect their bombers from the fast and manoeuvrable Zero fighters of the Japanese and the torpedoes fired by the bombers were slow and inaccurate. To set against these disadvantages Nimitz had one priceless asset: he had foreknowledge of the Japanese plans thanks to American code-breakers, whereas the Japanese remained ignorant of the whereabouts and composition of his force. The Japanese carriers launched their aircraft against Midway, but when the aircraft returned and landed on the decks to rearm and refuel, the bombers of the American carriers lurking undetected to the north struck. In a few minutes the carriers were turned into raging infernos. The Japanese Navy Minister later said, 'After Midway, I was certain that there was no chance of success.' The damage done was irreparable. Thirty per cent of the six hundred highly trained carrier pilots were killed and 40 per cent more were injured: they were very difficult to replace. It took Japanese shipyards a year to build replacements for the four lost carriers, whilst the Battle of Midway initiated a period during which aircraft were lost at a rate double that at which they were produced.

The Battle of Midway marks the point at which the Japanese lost control of the sea. This occurred even before American material superiority could be made to tell. Things could only get worse for the Japanese as American submarines sank their merchant shipping: by mid-1945 three quarters of it had been lost. Japan was never able to develop the vast area over which it had won control into an economic power to rival that of the United States. Instead, as the USA mobilized its immense resources for the purpose of making

Battle of Midway June 1942

Japan loses control of the sea

war, the imbalance of power between the two nations became ever more extreme. The measure of US material superiority is suggested by the statistics for the construction of aircraft carriers. In 1943-4 the Japanese built seven; the Americans built ninety.

The Americans simultaneously pursued several different strategies aiming at the defeat of Japan. General MacArthur insisted on the importance of re-taking the Philippines, which was finally achieved after a long campaign in 1944-5 and at enormous cost to the inhabitants. The Americans kept hoping that Chiang Kai-shek's Chinese would do to the Japanese what Stalin's Russians did to the Germans. This was the reason why they wanted to supply him from India and hence supported Slim's Burma campaign, which removed the Japanese threat to the route. Unfortunately, their efforts to reform Chiang's regime and army proved vain and the Generalissimo remained more interested in keeping the Communists under Mao Zedong in check than in fighting the Japanese. Much the most fruitful of the strategies pursued was that adopted by the navy, essentially an 'island-hopping' strategy. The Japanese were forced to disperse their forces by garrisoning large numbers of Pacific islands which could otherwise be used as bases against them. The Americans could concentrate on capturing certain key islands and thereby could approach more closely the Japanese home islands until they acquired a base from which they could strike at them. By mid-1944 the Americans were in a position to attack the Mariana Islands. Off the island of Saipan the greatest naval battle of the war was fought. Japan lost 475 aircraft and three aircraft carriers. The Americans had not only crippled Japanese air and sea power, but had acquired bases from which bombs could be rained down on Japanese cities.

Philippines re-taken

Americans attack the Mariana Islands

6. The Atom Bomb and the Surrender of Japan, August 1945

By mid-1944 it was obvious to all significant Japanese leaders that the Pacific War was lost. Nonetheless, the Japanese soldiers continued to fight with fanatical determination and their political and military leaders encouraged them to do so in the hope of negotiating terms that in reality were not achievable. The Japanese calculated that the Americans, with their abhorrence of heavy casualties, would eventually baulk at paying the price in blood which the total defeat of Japan would exact. They wholly misunderstood American determination to punish their nation, which had flouted international law by its attack on Pearl Harbor without so much as a declaration of war and had revealed itself as barbarous and uncivilized by its brutal conduct in China. There was no chance that the Japanese would be allowed to hang on to Korea and Manchuria, as even the most pacific of the Japanese demanded. Besides, no Japanese minister was prepared to step out of line and break with the militarist fanatics, who had a habit of assassinating anyone who did. As the months went by, the Japanese leaders came no nearer to acknowledging the realities of their desperate position.

In the last days of April 1945 Harry Truman, US President since Roosevelt's death earlier in the month, was told of a new factor in the situation, the successful development of a new, uniquely destructive weapon, the atomic bomb. The possibility of such a weapon had been recognized by all the main belligerent powers. In April 1940 a committee of top British scientists had been set up to evaluate the possibility of producing a bomb in time for use during the war. Its positive conclusion, announced in mid-1941, led to the decision to proceed. The British, however, were compelled to recognize in mid-1942 that they lacked the resources to develop the bomb speedily and it was the Americans who took over the project. In the spring of 1945, the Manhattan Project, as it was code-named, came to fruition and in July a successful test was carried out in the New Mexican desert.

The capitulation of Germany on 8 May drew from Tokyo merely a statement of its increased determination to fight on. The Japanese government was known by the Americans to be attempting to play Stalin off against the USA, which further sharpened American impatience. The Americans had won the war in the Pacific, but, frustratingly, the enemy refused to make peace. Dropping the atom bomb on Japan looked a useful means to get the Japanese to see reason at last. There was some urgency about the matter. The Americans had earlier sought to persuade Stalin to join in the war against Japan. When he was at last ready to do so, the Americans were unsure that they still wanted him to participate. Their experience of his policies in Europe made it seem likely that the price of his intervention would be high. The use of the bomb was likely to speed up Japan's surrender and reduce the significance of any military effort which Stalin might have time to make and the extent of the rewards that he could claim. Hence, the use of the bomb had as its primary purpose the extraction from the Japanese of a decision for unconditional surrender, but it was also meant to strengthen America's position against the Soviets.

Japan refuses to make peace

The Potsdam Declaration of 26th July 1945 made the American position quite clear: the Japanese must surrender unconditionally or face 'prompt and utter destruction.' The Japanese had no idea what exactly the words meant and the Americans made no move to enlighten them, since part of the point of dropping an atom bomb was to administer an immense shock that might at last make the Japanese face reality. On 6 August an atom bomb was dropped on Hiroshima, chosen because it had not been much bombed already. Out of 76,000 buildings, 70,000 were destroyed; perhaps 70,000 people died immediately, and more would die in following years from the effects of radiation. The decision-making machinery of the Japanese government worked as slowly as ever, so that there was still no decision to give in. As a result, a second bomb was dropped as planned three days later, this time on Nagasaki, killing at least 30,000 more people. Shortly beforehand, the USSR had declared war on Japan and invaded Manchuria.

The Potsdam Declaration July 1945

Atomic bomb dropped on Hiroshima

Second bomb dropped on Nagasaki

Even after the disasters of August 1945, there were those in the Japanese military who preferred to fight on, but the Emperor threw his weight behind the peace party and made possible its success.

Japan surrenders unconditionally August 1945

Japan surrendered unconditionally, relying on American goodwill to secure the survival of the imperial throne. Conspiracies to sabotage the peace were foiled, though a number of Japanese military men preferred suicide to what they regarded as the dishonour of surrender.

Asian casualties of Pacific War

It was principally Asians who lost their lives in the armed conflicts in eastern Asia between 1937 and 1945. To gain and defend its conquests Japan sacrificed about 2.69 million people, but the Chinese suffered far more, with losses of at least fifteen and possibly as many as fifty million. Up to five million inhabitants of South-East Asia are thought to have perished. By contrast, British and American losses were light: 30,000 British died, many as prisoners of the Japanese, and around 90,000 Americans. Most of the conflicts in which the Americans were engaged required huge expenditure on machinery, especially ships and aeroplanes, but consumed relatively few American lives.

The Pacific War occasioned by Japan's bid for empire is usually lumped together with the wars in Europe and northern Africa brought about by the expansionism of Germany and Italy as the Second World War. Yet the Pacific War had little in common with the other wars, except that Britain (because its Empire was world-wide) and America (because it is a Pacific and an Atlantic power) took part in them all. Japan and Germany were supposed to be allies and Germany followed Japan's lead in going to war with America in December 1941, but there was no co-ordination of military or naval effort. The Japanese and German wars coincided in time, but remained otherwise distinct conflicts.

Japan enjoyed an impressive run of victories in 1941-2, which astounded and terrified the world. Yet its successes were mostly achieved against fading colonial powers distracted by more pressing concerns or against the disorganized, disunited and still largely un-modernized power of China. The USA was a different matter. It had ten times the industrial might of Japan and to defeat it the Japanese could rely only on the fighting spirit of which they were so proud. The samurai ethos was not enough to overcome the Americans and it became the greatest obstacle to Japan's exit from the war while their cities were still intact.

VIII

LABOUR'S CREATIVE PERIOD, 1945-1947

1. Labour's Election Victory of 1945

EVER since the overthrow of Chamberlain in May 1940, all three main parties had been in a coalition led by Winston Churchill, and normal party politics had been suspended. There had been no general election since 1935. By-elections were held during the war, but official candidates from the main parties had not stood against each other. The coalition had been held together by the general agreement that winning the war was the overwhelming national priority. Once the war was won, then, the reason for the coalition's existence would cease to exist. After the First World War, government by coalition had continued till 1922, but that coalition was felt by many people, especially those of progressive opinions, to have failed the nation by failing to deliver social reform. Members of the Labour Party were determined not to become prisoners of the Conservatives, as the coalition Liberals of 1918-22 seemed to have been. There was pressure on the party leaders to end the coalition as soon as possible. VE Day (Victory in Europe) was celebrated on 8 May. Churchill urged the Labour ministers to remain in his government until the defeat of Japan and Attlee and Bevin received his request sympathetically. In the end, though, pressure from the party proved irresistible and on 20 May the Labour ministers brought the coalition to an end by resigning from it.

The Coalition government was immediately succeeded by an interim Conservative government, which ruled until a general election could be held. It was an election which most Labour leaders expected to lose. They recalled the precedent of 1918, when Lloyd George had won a huge majority as the man who had won the war, and they assumed that the Conservatives would coast to victory on the coat tails

Coalition Government

VE Day 1945

Labour ministers resign from the coalition

Interim Conservative government

Gallup poll predicts Labour victory

of their leader, Churchill. In the spring of 1945 a Gallup poll produced a lead for Labour over the Conservatives of 20 per cent and thereafter a series of polls predicted a gradually diminishing, but still substantial lead for Labour. In 1945, however, politicians had not yet learnt to take opinion polls seriously.

In 1945 Churchill's war record did not prove to be an election winner. Perhaps this was partly because the Second World War ended in a different way from the First. The First World War ended suddenly and unexpectedly and the election of 1918 took place while the War was still at the forefront of everyone's mind, but when the election of 1945 was held, the outcome of the Second World War had not been in doubt for a long time. The minds of electors were less preoccupied with the War than with what might come after it. If domestic reform was the main item on the agenda, then Churchill's performance in the War, admirable though most people thought it was, might not be considered relevant to the way they cast their votes. Churchill had in any case acquired a status as a national figure, not as a party hero. In the 1930s his had been a voice crying in the wilderness, ignored by the appeasers in his party. The Conservative leaders of the 1930s were seen by many as 'guilty men', whose craven foreign policy had let the country down and built Hitler up. In 1945 people were not necessarily repudiating Churchill when they repudiated a Conservative Party which had let the country down in the 1930s. In 1918, by contrast, no blame could be attached to the Conservatives for the recent war.

Conservative Party associated with appeasement

The Labour leaders came out of the war with impeccable patriotic credentials. Victory was due to them as much as to the Conservatives. The government positions in which they had laboured were primarily ones connected with the home front. Ernest Bevin had been a successful Minister of Labour, who had geared industrial production to the tasks of keeping the armed services adequately supplied. Herbert Morrison had a good record as Home Secretary, a post which put him in charge of home defence and repairing the ravages of the Blitz. The Cabinet Reconstruction Committee concerned itself with policies for full employment and freeing the regions from dependence on single, often declining industries. It was dominated by Labour ministers such as Attlee and Morrison and included only 'Rab' Butler among prominent Conservatives. The war had produced a great expansion of officialdom and a great deal of central planning covering major industries, food distribution and so on. There was growing enthusiasm for state planning, which was seen as the way to achieve the desirable objectives considered by the Reconstruction Committee. An ambitious scheme for compulsory social insurance to protect individuals from misfortune from the cradle to the grave was published in the Beveridge Report of 1942 and aroused great interest and excitement. Thanks in part to their ministers' wartime roles, the Labour Party looked a lot more likely to deliver reform than the Conservatives were. The Conservatives were associated with what were seen as the lamentable failures of the inter-war years, especially the failure to eliminate the scourge of unemployment. There was widespread determination that the new post-war period should not be like the period after the First World War, when the rewards of victory had failed to materialise. It seemed time to trust a new set of politicians to deliver them.

The Labour Party has always had a very close relationship with the trade unions and this connection was especially intimate in the war, when Ernest Bevin, General Secretary of the Transport and General Workers Union (TGWU) and Minister of Labour, bestrode the party and the union movement like a colossus. The number of trade unionists had increased rapidly during the war, bringing added strength and money to the party. Bevin had brought union leaders into close association with the government, which they helped to direct production and to control the labour market. Labour relations had not always been harmonious at local level, but it did look as if Bevin could deliver a partnership between unions, private industry and government. Such a partnership would avoid regrettable incidents like the General Strike of 1926 and go far towards assuring Britain's

Clement Attlee and Herbert Morrison

Beveridge Report 1942

Trade union relations with Labour

prosperity and success as an industrial power. Here was another reason for voting Labour.

Churchill called the election for 5 July, allowing six weeks for the campaign. It was agreed that Churchill's towering personality far outshone that of the reserved and uncharismatic Attlee, who was accused by one supporter of lacking 'a sense of the dramatic, the power to give a lead, the ability to reach out to the masses'. It could be that Attlee's reticence helped him by making Churchill's charge that Labour might introduce a sort of Gestapo (the Nazi secret police) into Britain, presumably under Attlee as Führer, seem all the more absurd. It was hard for their opponents to present Labour as dangerous or extreme, as had sometimes been attempted between the wars, given the record of its coalition ministers. Clearly, Attlee's personality did not much damage his party, for when the votes were counted, Labour was found to have won by a landslide. Labour gained over 200 seats, ending with 393 to only 210 for the Conservatives. In England the Liberals were almost wiped out: their 12 seats were almost all won in the Celtic fringe. The Labour vote was over eight percentage points higher than the Conservative: Labour had 48 per cent of the vote to the Conservatives' 39.6 per cent. Labour did well in every type of seat, including suburban and rural ones. Never before (and never again) was it so obviously a national party. It was therefore able to proceed to form the first Labour government with an overall majority in the House of Commons.

Labour
landslide
victory

2. The Nationalization Programme

In its short history the Labour Party had been plagued by quarrels and splits; the collapse of Ramsay MacDonald's government in 1931 was only the most dramatic of these. The election victory of 1945, however, ushered in a period of party harmony. Through its years in power, 1945-51, the party steadily increased its membership, which stood at over a million individuals by 1952. Quite remarkably, the party lost only one seat at a by-election to a Conservative during its six years in office. Hence party morale remained high and the team of ministers remained united until the significant resignations of April 1951.

The Labour movement was dominated by the Cabinet. Attlee headed it as Prime Minister. His modest manner and introverted personality hid a will to power, which was most evident in the first eighteen months of his premiership, when he made much of the running on foreign and Indian affairs. Thereafter his position was unassailable, except briefly in the crisis of 1947. Attlee depended heavily on the unwavering support of Ernest Bevin, who possessed in full measure the flamboyance and imposing presence which his chief lacked. Bevin's pivotal position in the government was due in part to his role as the spokesman of the trade unions, but he also proved perhaps the most dominating Foreign Secretary since the time of Palmerston. Bevin was probably given the Foreign Office to keep him out of the way of his rival Herbert Morrison, the third key figure in the government. Morrison was important in keeping the parliamentary party contented and in framing the government's programmes. He was less impressive as director of economic planning for the first two years of the government's life.

Morrison was especially important when the government came to implement Labour's commitment to nationalization, which it had made central to its aspirations in the manifesto of 1945. Labour had written a pledge to bring about public ownership of the means of production and distribution into its constitution in 1918. Only in the 1930s had the meaning of this commitment begun to be spelt out, and by 1945 a list of industries and services to be nationalised had been drawn up. There remained the question of the form that nationalization was to take. On this issue the crucial thinking had been done by Morrison. In 1931 he had set up the London Passenger Transport Board and in the following years he drew from it a blueprint for public corporations which could run those industries ear-marked

Attlee becomes Prime Minister

Ernest Bevin heads Foreign Office

National-ization

London Passenger Transport Board

for public ownership. The London Passenger Transport Board seemed a model of efficient public management. Composed of public bureaucrats, it operated without political interference and was not beholden to vested interests such as trade unions. Morrison's model seemed a serviceable one.

Later generations of left-wing politicians were sometimes to regret that the Labour government had not been more ambitious in its nationalization programme of the 1940s and adopted a model which offered a degree of industrial democracy or workers' control. Yet in 1945 the only model on offer was that of Herbert Morrison, who alone had tried to work out what public ownership might mean in practice. Furthermore, the trade union representatives of the workers had absolutely no wish to get involved in management. They were far more comfortable with their traditional role of defending the wage-earners against their employers, a role which continued to be relevant in nationalized industries. They were content simply to assume that nationalized industries would be kinder to their workers.

The purpose of nationalization which was stressed at the time was economic efficiency, not social revolution. Industries such as coal and the railways were believed to have failed the nation and to be in need of reorganization. Institutions such as the Bank of England and new industries such as civil aviation needed to be integrated into a national policy of investment and re-equipment. The war had given people great faith in planning and in non-partisan experts. Labour's nationalization programme embodied this faith, which was so general that the programme ran into remarkably little opposition either within the Labour Party or from the Conservatives. The measures of nationalization were accepted more readily too because the Labour government did not proceed by robbing anyone of their property. Shareholders in the industries to be taken into public ownership were compensated quite generously.

Four major measures of nationalization were piloted through Parliament during the first year of Labour rule. The Bank of England

Advisory role of non-partisan experts

Bank of England nationalized

was nationalized; Cable and Wireless became a government-owned company with the aim of co-ordinating telecommunications between Britain and the Dominions; and in the area of civil aviation the government completed the integration of smaller companies into two state-controlled companies, British European Airways (BEA) and British Overseas Airways Corporation (BOAC), a development already begun by the National government in 1940. The only one of the measures to arouse much excitement was the nationalization of the coal mines. No one was prepared to defend the mine-owners, given the dismal record of industrial relations within the industry. Memories of the General Strike and the victimization which followed it were still green. The mine-owners were vulnerable too on another front: the industry was very inefficient. This had a serious effect on the whole economy, since coal was still the main source of power and a vital export. Labour's solution to these problems was botched. The structure of the nationalized industry was over-centralized and after the euphoria which greeted the achievement of nationalization, it became clear that industrial disturbances had by no means become past history.

In 1947-8 other measures of nationalization followed. The gas and electricity industries were brought into national ownership. The nationalization of the railways seemed no more than a further concentration of ownership and control, completing what the Lloyd George coalition had done in 1921. The attempted nationalization of road haulage, however, was highly controversial. The rationale was to achieve an integrated system of road and rail transport, avoiding duplication and wasteful competition. Yet the measure would have involved nationalizing hundreds of thousands of small road transport operators: this was no mere nationalization of a natural monopoly, as in the case of gas or rail transport. In order to get the rest of its Transport Bill through, the government was compelled to yield over the small road operators. Perhaps this was a sign that nationalization was nearing its limit of acceptability.

Cable and Wireless

BEA and BOAC

Coal Industry

Between 1945 and 1948 the Labour government had put through a huge programme of public ownership, involving almost one fifth of the economy. For Labour MPs the programme was very important in giving them the sense that they were steadily building socialism. The sense of momentum helped to keep the party contented and united in its common enterprise. Few of the measures were of interest to the Labour masses, though the miners' union leaders viewed nationalization of the mines as a culminating triumph in their long struggle against hated mine-owners and railwaymen were enthusiastic supporters of the nationalization of the railways. Nationalization happened chiefly because the political and technocratic elites had lost faith in *laisser faire*, the idea that businessmen are best left alone to run the economy. State control had come to seem not only more benevolent, but also more efficient. If it could help Britain to win a war, perhaps it could also help Britain to thrive in peace. It is highly significant that the enactment of this programme was relatively uncontroversial between the main parties. No doubt, Conservative acquiescence owed something to the trauma of their defeat in the election of 1945, from which they were still recovering. It was also the case that Labour was able to build on precedents, such as the creation of BOAC in 1940, or the municipal socialism which had already brought gas in many places into public, if not national, ownership. Above all, however, forward-looking Conservatives, hardly less than Labour, were affected by the mood of the time and that mood favoured state control and direction. The nationalizing measures of Labour's first years were not undone when the Conservatives returned to office. Like much else that Labour did after 1945, these measures were accepted by a national consensus, which lasted till the 1980s.

Conservative acquiescence in Labour programme

That the nationalization measures of 1945-8 were for so long accepted indicates that, despite criticisms, they were generally felt to be a success. By 1952 the National Coal Board was in profit and even winning export markets. Thanks in part to a programme of capital

National Coal Board

investment, production rose from 190 million tons in 1946 to 222 million by 1951 and productivity per shift worked reached its highest level ever. Working conditions were greatly improved and though there was some trouble in the South Yorkshire and South Wales coalfields in the later 1940s, labour relations had much improved since nationalization, whilst labour relations in the other newly nationalized industries were generally excellent. On the other hand, the British industrial scene had certainly not been transformed. Labour relations, even if better for the moment, were still conducted on the old basis which set bosses, even those of nationalized industries, against unions representing the workforce. There was no attempt to achieve even integration among the nationalized industries: each was run as a separate enterprise and no integrated transport or energy policy emerged.

Lack of integrated policies

3. The Social Policies of the Labour Government

When in the election campaign of 1950 the Labour government came to defend its record to the nation, it chose to dwell not on its programme of nationalization, but on the creation of a welfare state. 'Labour has honoured the pledge it made in 1945 to make social security the birthright of every citizen. Today destitution has been banished. The best medical care is available to everybody in the land,' boasted the manifesto of 1950.

Creation of the Welfare State

The Welfare State was not the creation of Labour alone. The foundations were laid by Lloyd George and the Liberals before 1914. Inter-war governments had greatly extended help for the unemployed. Above all, during the War in 1942, William Beveridge, a Liberal, produced his famous report calling for a comprehensive system of social security, designed to safeguard the welfare of individuals afflicted by the misfortunes which researchers had long since identified as the main causes of poverty: sickness, disability, unemployment and old age. The Labour Party appropriated the report, which seemed to

Beveridge Report 1942

echo some of the party's own policy statements, and in effect incorporated it into its manifesto of 1945.

A Welsh miner, James Griffiths, became Minister of National Insurance, charged with realising Beveridge's vision. Unlike the earlier social insurance schemes, this one was comprehensive, in that one compulsory flat-rate contribution bought protection against all the main causes of poverty; it was universal, in that everyone was covered; and it was considerably more generous. Maternity benefits, widows' benefits and family allowances (at 5s per child) stopped up various gaps in the provisions, which were designed to provide for everyone a national minimum standard of living. Unfortunately, thanks to Treasury parsimony, the benefits provided proved to be nearly a third below what was needed for subsistence. In 1948, however, the National Assistance Act was passed to provide a safety net for the poor and exorcise memories of the poverty which some sections of the community had experienced in the 1930s. Assistance had to be means-tested, but it was no longer whole households, but individuals who were means-tested, so that Aneurin Bevan, Labour Minister of Health, could declare: 'I have spent many years of my life in fighting the means test. Now we have practically ended it.'

Compre-hensive National Insurance

Maternity, Widow and family allowances

National Assistance Act 1948

'Nye' Bevan was known as a firebrand from the mining valleys of South Wales, but in 1945 he was given the task of constructing the National Health Service (NHS), which was seen as an essential adjunct to state health insurance. Bevan aimed to create a system which provided everyone with free health care, the costs of which would be funded from national taxation, not from an insurance scheme. All hospitals were to be nationalized: they were to be run by appointed regional boards accountable to the Ministry of Health. Bevan met opposition from two sources. Herbert Morrison spoke for those who regretted the demise of hospitals run by local authorities and were apprehensive about the state-controlled monolith which Bevan was in the process of creating. The concern of the time was uniformity and efficiency, not responsiveness, and Morrison's reservations were

Aneurin 'Nye' Bevan and the National Health Service

158

overridden. One of the major changes of the 1940s was the conversion of Labour from a party which favoured local initiative, whether in running hospitals, or supplying gas and electricity, or relieving poverty, to a party which entrusted the implementation of its policies to a hugely enlarged state bureaucracy. Bevan had a far tougher battle with the British Medical Association representing the doctors, who feared that instead of being partners in privately run practices, they would be reduced to the position of salaried state employees. After a two-year battle, Bevan finally managed to reassure them, and the NHS went ahead in 1948, covering the vast majority of the population. The National Health Service did not cease to be controversial, largely because its appetite for resources constantly outran estimates, but most of the essential principles on which it was based were to be generally accepted for the next half-century and beyond.

NHS created 1948

Bevan was given responsibility not only for health, but also for housing, which probably overloaded him, since this too was an immensely challenging task. It was reckoned that a million houses were required for working-class occupants, not to mention the bomb damage to be put right and the slum clearance that would have at some stage to be restarted. There were severe shortages of everything: of money to finance house-building; of materials, which were also needed for factories and schools and sometimes had to be paid for in scarce dollars; and of labour. Bevan determined to restrict private house-building and to pour resources into local-authority housing. He wanted the housing to be permanent and of high standard, with lavatories upstairs and down and a generous provision of floor space, between 750 and 900 square feet. He was very much against temporary 'pre-fabs' (prefabricated houses), which he dismissed as 'rabbit-hutches'. 'We shall be judged for a year or two by the number of houses we build. We shall be judged in ten years' time by the type of houses we build,' Bevan said. He also hoped to end social segregation and mix the classes together, but it was never clear how he proposed to achieve this objective.

Housing policy under Bevan

Slum clearances

Pre-fab housing

Progress in dealing with the housing problem was at first very slow and the government was embarrassed by direct action by homeless people who squatted in empty buildings in London and elsewhere, drawing attention to the inadequacies of the government's record and then making it look heartless when it had them evicted. Yet by September 1948 Bevan could announce that three quarters of a million **New homes** new homes had been provided since the end of the war, half of them **announced** permanent new houses, the rest pre-fabs and other temporary homes and repaired houses. Somewhat erratic progress continued to the end of the Labour government in 1951, with a different minister injecting new energy into the programme in Labour's final year. The housing problem had most certainly not been solved by Labour, but an enormous impetus had been given to the public provision of housing for the working class, many of whom had lacked adequate housing at affordable rents. The emphasis on local-authority provision was distinctive in post-war Europe: by the end of the 1970s a third of Britain's entire housing stock was run by local authorities. This was, however, not yet the age of the tower-block. Local authorities were reluctant to build flats, preferring 'cottage-style' housing. In London this reluctance was to some degree overcome, since borough councils were persuaded that flats alone would permit borough populations to be maintained at existing levels. Even in London, though, the height of blocks of flats was kept low by later standards.

The Labour Minister of Education was 'Red' Ellen Wilkinson, **Ellen** red not only because of the colour of her hair, but also because of her **Wilkinson,** political stance in the 1930s, especially her organization of the Jarrow **Minister of** Hunger March. Despite Treasury parsimony, she managed to get free **Education** school milk introduced (a third of a pint per school day) for young pupils; she raised the school-leaving age to 15; and she got a school-building programme under way. Her work at the Ministry, however, failed to shape the future in the way that Griffiths or Bevan did in **The Butler** connection with other aspects of Labour's social policies. The Butler **Act 1944** Act of 1944 had laid it down that secondary education should be provided for everyone, whereas previously 80 per cent of children had stayed on in primary education until they reached the school-leaving age. The Act assumed, but did not require, that secondary education would have a tripartite structure. Selective grammar schools would deliver an academic curriculum enabling pupils to satisfy entrance requirements for universities. There would be technical schools with a vocational emphasis. Everyone else would attend secondary modern schools. In theory, the three different types of school would enjoy parity of esteem. Wilkinson positively encouraged tripartism. She envisaged a new generation of bright, self-motivated working-class children going to grammar schools, receiving an education that would make them the equals of products of Eton and Westminster, and from there advancing to leading positions in the country. She hoped that they would not be kept back, as she felt she had been, by waiting for the slower and less keen students in unselective classes. The system did not work out as she had hoped, especially in that very few technical schools were set up and grammar schools came to enjoy a monopoly of esteem. Even before 1951, some in the Labour party expressed fundamental reservations about the whole tripartite system. Opportunities for a small minority of bright working-class children seemed to have been bought at the expense of the great majority, while so far from advancing a classless society, the system seemed to reinforce existing class divisions.

Mandatory Secondary Education

Grammar, Technical and Secondary Modern Schools

One of the key responsibilities assumed by Labour's Welfare State was the achievement of full employment. Inevitably, there were difficulties early on, as the number of troops was run down from five to one million and industry in some places revived only slowly. There were fears that the scourge of unemployment might be reviving, as the numbers of the jobless temporarily reached a million in the winter of 1947. The crisis of 1947, however, was followed by a period of rapid industrial expansion and unemployment more or less disappeared. Circumstances were favourable: the economies of potential rivals such as Germany took time to recover from wartime devastation. Yet

Goal of full employment

Industrial expansion

government policy also played a positive role. Every effort was made to diversify and modernize industry in such areas as central Scotland, South Wales and the north-east, where the decline of old staple industries had produced high unemployment between the wars. Firms were coerced into starting up in these areas rather than in the south-east or east Midlands by the use of Industrial Development Certificates. Interest-free loans and remission of taxes were used as inducements to industry to locate in the Development Areas. As a result, by 1949 even in these difficult areas unemployment was under 5 per cent, and the national level was under 2 per cent. In fact, shortage of labour and difficulties in getting it to where it was needed were the chief worries of industrialists and economic ministers in these years.

Full employment attained

Attainment of full employment was perhaps the proudest boast of Clement Attlee's government.

4. Society and Culture after the War

Post-war austerity

The advent of a Labour government did nothing to relieve the drabness and restrictions of wartime Britain. Britain's trade had to be brought back into balance as fast as possible by limiting imports and launching an export drive. Rationing therefore had to continue into the post-war years and was even extended when bread was rationed for the first time in 1946. People had hoped that after winning the war, they would be free to enjoy life again, but many things were in even shorter supply than they had been during the war. The post-war period was a time of austerity. Perhaps it is not surprising that

Post-war Emigration

there was considerable emigration to the Dominions and to Southern Rhodesia.

Food shortages

The loudest complaints seem to have been about the food situation. Despite rationing, food was often in short supply and housewives had to spend a lot of time queuing and returning to shops more than once a day in the hope that more food would have been delivered. Though it was not difficult to procure the components of the basic diet, the more palatable foods were often hard to obtain. Production, prices and distribution were all controlled in the name of fair shares for all, but, of course, there was a flourishing black market and consequent complaint about unfairness. Government ministers did their best to support the apparatus of control by emphasising the immorality of circumventing the regulations, which was denounced as a 'social crime'. The government cultivated a puritanical, morally earnest image, embodied in the prim Prime Minister and the ascetic Sir Stafford Cripps, by 1947 the government's rising star. It is doubtful, however, whether the government's exhortations had much effect in preventing people from resorting to the black market, occasionally at least, to ease the burden of controls on their families.

Stafford Cripps

All sorts of commodities were unavailable, with the result that many things were in short supply, such as clothes and cars, and choice was very limited. All cars were black, for example, and new furniture could be purchased only from the government-sponsored Utility range. Where there are controls, there will be people who specialize in avoiding them for a profit and in these years such men were commonly known as 'spivs'. They were said to be instantly recognizable: clad in coats with wide lapels and padded shoulders, sporting ties with huge knots, and with hair parted in the middle and pencil moustache. By 1949, however, the spivs' opportunities were beginning to decline as Harold Wilson, President of the Board of Trade, set alight a series of what he called 'bonfires' of controls, which at last took many goods off the ration: all clothes rationing, for example, ended in 1949.

'Spivs'

The urgent need to cut imports which had perpetuated rationing also affected government policy regarding agriculture. This industry had suffered badly in the 1930s, when world agricultural prices had been low, but had revived during the war when Britain had been forced to aim at self-sufficiency in food production. Every effort had therefore been made to maximise production by modernising agricultural technology and farmers had become national heroes for their contribution to Britain's survival. Under the ex-miner Tom

Modern-
ization of
agriculture

Williams, appointed Minister of Agriculture, the same aims were pursued in peacetime. Farmers were assured markets for most of their produce and prices were guaranteed. The annual price review was agreed in consultation with representatives of the farmers in the National Farmers' Union. Grants were readily available for modernization and the government ran a scientific advisory service. It is not surprising that Williams became known as 'the Farmers' Friend'. The farmers did what Williams expected them to do and vastly

Food production increased

increased food production, which in 1950 was 46 per cent above the pre-war level. The price for this achievement was not paid by the consumer, who was cushioned by large food subsidies, but by the taxpayers who paid for the subsidies. There turned out to be other consequences too, though in the 1940s hardly anyone noticed them. Industrial farming was bad for wildlife and often for the landscape, as

Damage to wildlife and the environment

miles of hedgerow were dug up and parts of the countryside began to resemble wheat-growing prairies. Modernization and mechanization also meant that fewer and fewer workers were needed on the land, so that rural society came under threat. This was the very moment when the people of Britain took more interest in village life than ever before, as was shown by the success of the long-running radio soap, *The Archers*, broadcast from 1950. Yet the country folk the programme celebrated were soon in danger of disappearing.

The situation in the countryside was not improved by the Town and Country Planning Act of 1944, which tried to protect the countryside from suburban and industrial development and thereby

Town and Country Planning Act 1944

risked depopulating it altogether. The Act also gave the authorities powers to implement a vision for the towns. One influential set of ideas derived from Ebenezer Howard, who, writing in 1898, wanted to disperse population from huge cities and create new, self-supporting towns of around 30,000 inhabitants of mixed social background. There people would live in a light, airy environment, surrounded by

The 'green belt'

a 'green belt' of land not built over. Following these ideas, two garden cities had been built in Hertfordshire. The Greater London Plan of

1945 envisaged the metropolis ringed by a substantial green belt with new towns beyond. Accordingly, the New Towns Act of 1946 provided for the building of eight new towns round London, including Crawley, Bracknell, Stevenage and Basildon, while another six were to be established near other great centres of population. The towns were to be managed by government-funded and appointed development corporations. Lewis Silkin, Minister of Town and Country Planning, voiced to the House of Commons his hope that 'We may well produce in the new towns a new type of citizen, a healthy, self-respecting dignified person with a sense of beauty, culture and civic pride.' By the end of the Labour government in 1951 progress with the new towns had been disappointingly slow and some of the hopes associated with them were not being fulfilled. In particular, there was difficulty in achieving the right balance between housing and industry, so that the new towns were tending to turn into dormitories for remote city centres. From the planners came another criticism. The new towns contained mainly low-rise housing, which was what their inhabitants said they wanted, but influential voices were increasingly raised in favour of high-rise blocks of flats, seen as less wasteful of money and land and, above all, as more 'modern'.

New Towns Act 1946

The first years after the war provided limited opportunities for architects, since resources had to be concentrated on domestic housing, schools and hospitals. At last in 1951 there arose a chance to design a whole area in order to achieve a strong impact on visitors. It was decided to mark the centenary of the Great Exhibition of 1851 with a new exhibition aiming to demonstrate that mid-20th-century Britons could be as innovative as their predecessors of a century earlier. Herbert Morrison, the politician in charge, believed that it would be 'a tonic for the nation'. In designing the exhibition space on a cleared bomb site, Hugh Casson determined to introduce the British public to modernism in architecture and to its linking of spaces and buildings. The potential of modern materials was illustrated by the Dome of Discovery, made of concrete and aluminium, and, most

Festival of Britain 1951

FESTIVAL OF BRITAIN COMMEMORATIVE STAMPS, 1951

adventurously, by the Skylon Tower, cigar-shaped and aluminium-clad, supported in the air by cables. The only building which survives on its original site is the Royal Festival Hall, for musical performances, described by one of the architects as 'an egg in a box', because the curved inner space is separate from the exterior walls. It later became the first post-war building to become Grade One listed. The main exhibition on the South Bank was visited by almost eight and a half million visitors.

Though the associated Battersea fun fair was just about enjoyment, essentially the Festival of Britain was part of the Labour government's high-minded attempt to raise the cultural level of the mass of the population. To the same end, the Arts Council was established to subsidize the arts through grants and loans and local councils were empowered to support the arts from the rates. The BBC was also anxious to sell high culture to the British public, especially through its Third Programme. All these initiatives had difficulty in reaching the working masses, but they helped to stimulate a boom in English music. The four great London orchestras – the Royal Philharmonic under Sir Thomas Beecham, the London Philharmonic, the London Symphony and the BBC Symphony – flourished and important orchestras were formed or re-formed elsewhere too, for example in Birmingham, Manchester and Scotland. The post-war years also saw

Arts Council established

the institution of the Edinburgh International Festival of Music and Drama and the Aldeburgh Festival. The latter was founded by Benjamin Britten, who acquired an international reputation as a composer, on a par with that which Elgar had earlier enjoyed. But Britten was not alone. Michael Tippett was in the process of achieving considerable fame and established figures such as Vaughan Williams found a new opening for composers by becoming involved in the writing of film music.

Edinburgh and Aldeburgh Festivals founded

The immediate post-war years were also the period in which major talents emerged in other arts. Henry Moore had developed many of the elements of his sculpture before the war. Returning to sculpture in 1943, he sculpted his serenely aloof *Madonna and Child* for St Matthew's Church, Northampton. Another favourite theme was the reclining figure set outside in a landscape, which he realised in his *Memorial Figure* in the garden at Dartington Hall. These tranquil, monumental figures could hardly be more different from the first important work of the painter Francis Bacon, who in 1945 exhibited *Three Figures at the Base of a Crucifixion*. The artist portrayed twisted and distorted figures, half-human, half-animal, which seem to writhe and shriek. This disturbing work evoked abuse when first exhibited, but eventually helped to win the artist an international reputation. Thanks to Bacon, Moore and another sculptor, Barbara Hepworth, Britain ceased to be a backwater where the visual arts were concerned. The government played a modest role in this, through Arts Council patronage of Moore, for example.

Most of the greatest novelists active immediately after the war were already well known. They included George Orwell, whose most enduring works, *Animal Farm* and *1984*, belong to these years. He had become concerned with the threat of totalitarian tyranny, which since his experiences in Catalonia during the Spanish Civil War he saw as coming chiefly from the Stalinist left. Graham Greene was another outstanding novelist of these years. His chief concern was the relationship between God and man, but he was adept too at evoking particular times and places. His *Heart of the Matter* recreates the atmosphere of a West African colony in the twilight of British colonial rule and *The End of the Affair* recalls wartime London.

Popular broadcasting

Reading was a popular pastime, but listening to the radio seems to have become yet more popular. The popular programmes were not intellectually demanding. *Dick Barton – Special Agent*, with a cliffhanger at the end of every episode, was listened to by fifteen million people each night, which made it the most popular regular

The Archers

programme of all. *The Archers*, the soap about a fictitious agricultural village called Ambridge, ranked highly too, while popular comedy programmes made the reputations of Frankie Howerd and Benny Hill. The BBC did not take the opportunity to educate its listeners in current affairs. It ran scared of political controversy, adopting the 'fourteen day gag', which meant that issues were not discussed during the fortnight before Parliament was due to discuss them. On the television the BBC was unwilling even to provide news bulletins, but then as late as 1948 under 5 per cent of homes possessed a TV set.

Advent of televison

By 1951 the advent of television was beginning to make inroads on cinema audiences. They peaked in 1946 at 1,635 million, which meant that on average everyone over fifteen went to the cinema once a week. During the war, Hollywood acquired practically a monopoly of the British screen: visions of an America untouched by war provided the perfect escape from war-weary Britain. After the war, a government anxious to keep imports low did what it could to stimulate a British film industry. The National Film Corporation financed Carol Reed's classic *The Third Man*, set in post-war Vienna under Allied

Ealing Film Studios

occupation and based on a screenplay by Graham Greene. The Ealing Film Studios made many successful films gently satirical of British ways, but British films of this period tended to lack the mass appeal of Hollywood or the artistic distinction of French and Italian films.

Television as yet provided no alternative to watching sporting fixtures live. After the war football once more attracted huge crowds. At Hampden Park, Glasgow in 1947, 134,000 watched Great Britain play the Rest of Europe. 'Britain must Beat Europe: Our Prestige at Stake' was the headline in the *Daily Express*. British prestige turned out to be safe on this occasion. Watching football was a communal activity and in the post-war years people still wanted to have their fun together with other people. This was the golden age of the holiday camp, associated above all with the figure of Billy Butlin. He had founded camps at Skegness and Clacton before the war, but several more were added once the war was over and Butlin became a wealthy man. His camps had begun by attracting people from the middle class, but soon they were taken over by working-class families. The change showed that the workers were becoming more affluent and now had the cash to take the family on an annual holiday.

Butlin's Holiday Camps

DATE SUMMARY

Britain and Overseas 1945-51

BRITAIN	OVERSEAS
1945 Labour Ministry (Attlee)	1945 Potsdam Conference
1946-50 Nationalization programmes	San Francisco Conference sets up United Nations
Education Act (1944) begins to be put into effect	
	1946 The 'Truman Doctrine' (Greece, Turkey)
	1947 India and Pakistan become independent Commonwealth countries
1948 National Insurance and National Health Acts come into effect	1948 Britain ends Palestine Mandate: Arab-Israeli war Treaty of Brussels
	1948-9 Berlin blockade; Allied air-lift
1949 Republic of Ireland established Parliament Act amended: powers of Lords Reduced	1949 North Atlantic Treaty Organization
	1950 Korean War begins

IX

CRISIS AND CONSOLIDATION, 1947-1951

1. The Crisis of 1947

THE winter weather of 1947 proved to be the worst of the 20th century. For eight weeks from 20 January the wind came from the north-east, bringing bitter cold with it. There were heavy snowfalls and, when finally the snow melted, there was widespread flooding. The bad weather came when there was already a looming fuel crisis. The power stations and domestic heating depended overwhelmingly on coal and not enough was being produced. The mines had problems with insufficient labour, which were made worse by the introduction of the Miners' Charter granting miners a five-day week. The wintry weather then made a bad situation far worse. Demand soared and the transportation of coal round the country was disrupted. By early February, many power stations had run out of fuel. Domestic consumers had to go without power for several hours a day and much of industry had to close down. At one stage over two million people were out of work as a result. The crisis did not show in a good light a government which prided itself on planning ahead.

The interruption of exports which resulted from the shutdown of the winter of 1947 exacerbated the problems which the government's economic policies were running into. In Labour's first two years, the Chancellor of the Exchequer was Hugh Dalton. He was determined to avoid the sort of policies pursued by the Lloyd George coalition after the First World War, which had led to a contraction of the economy and high unemployment. He kept interest rates low and he made money available for a variety of objectives which he regarded as desirable: he subsidized food; he provided money to peg council house rents at a low level; he financed family allowances; and he assisted development areas. The expansion of the economy over which Dalton

Marginal notes: *Worst winter on record 1947* · *Fuel crisis and power shortages*

170

presided led to a greater demand for American food and raw materials. The demand could be met only because of the large American loan negotiated in 1945, which gave Britain the necessary dollars. The loan was supposed to last until 1951, but by 1947 it began to run out at an alarming rate. A rise in American prices and the collapse of exports during the fuel crisis made the situation much worse.

Dalton was still optimistic when he presented his budget in April 1947, but signs of a major crisis were already evident. The volume of exports fell and there was a huge imbalance in Britain's trade with America: over 42 per cent of imports came from the dollar area, but only 14 per cent of exports went there. In these already desperate circumstances, there loomed the prospect of 'convertibility'. In order to get the American loan in 1945, Britain had been obliged to agree that from 15 July 1947 all those holding pounds should be able to convert them into dollars. In the weeks after 15th July, holders of pounds around the world rushed to exchange pounds for dollars. Britain's dollar reserves rapidly became depleted and what remained of the American loan drained away. National bankruptcy loomed.

Trade deficit with USA

In the crisis of the summer of 1947, the government panicked. The Prime Minister seemed out of his depth and offered no leadership. Morrison was ill with heart trouble and Bevin's energy was fully absorbed by foreign policy. Finally, the Cabinet took the decision to end convertibility and the Americans were induced to agree to its suspension on 'an emergency and temporary' basis. In fact, convertibility had been permanently abandoned, since it was accepted that the pound was too weak for any further experiment. The immediate crisis ended.

Con-vertibility abandoned

There could be no return to Dalton's former cheerful optimism and expansionism. Great efforts to reduce imports paid for in dollars would be necessary. Food imports would therefore have to be reduced, which meant reductions of basic rations in a range of foodstuffs, such as meat, fats and sugar. Consumer purchasing power would also have to be reduced, and a start was made in Dalton's last budget of

November 1947. Dalton's authority had been severely undermined, since the crisis was seen as the outcome of his policies. An indiscretion in connection with the budget, when he revealed details in advance to a journalist, led to his resignation. His replacement was Sir Stafford Cripps, who had emerged from the crisis of the summer with his reputation intact.

Dalton replaced by Stafford Cripps

The crisis of 1947 also briefly shook the position of Attlee, who was urged to resign as Prime Minister by Cripps. Cripps' proposal that Bevin should take over instead was undermined by Bevin's refusal to agree. What emerged in the end was a ministerial reshuffle, which brought to prominence a younger generation of Labour politicians, such as Harold Wilson, who became President of the Board of Trade, and Hugh Gaitskell, the new Minister of Fuel and Power. The main beneficiary of the crisis of 1947, however, was Cripps, who took over powers to direct the economy from Morrison, whose burdens needed to be reduced to save his health. When Cripps took over the Treasury as well in November, he was indisputably the dominant figure in domestic policy. Attlee, though still Prime Minister, was diminished somewhat. The style and image of the government were associated with Cripps, while Attlee worked in the background as chairman and co-ordinator.

Harold Wilson, President of the Board of Trade

2. The Ascendancy of Sir Stafford Cripps

Sir Stafford Cripps was born into a Conservative, High Church family, but he became an enthusiastic socialist during a successful career at the bar. Initially attracted by the far left, he was expelled from the Parliamentary Labour Party in 1939. During the war, however, he moved to a centrist position, as he proved during his successful career at the Board of Trade between 1945 and 1947. During the crisis of 1947, when everyone else seemed to panic, Cripps impressed by what Gaitskell later called 'his amazingly keen intelligence and superb self-confidence.' His indomitable will

SIR STAFFORD CRIPPS AND GANDHI, MARCH 1942

promised to re-energize a government which, after the bruising events of 1947, seemed to have lost much of its own self-confidence and sense of direction. He had wide support. Business and the City felt safe under his rule, but he also had warm relations with leftists such as Bevan, sharing their commitment to social spending on health and housing. The Cabinet acquiesced in his assumption of enormous power over the economy and finances and gave him solid support. He exuded an air of moral rectitude, rather as Gladstone had, and as in the case of Gladstone, some people, Churchill for example, found this insufferable. 'There, but for the grace of God, goes God,' his critics gibed. He was a deeply committed High Anglican who lived a life of discipline and austerity. He was a teetotaller and a vegetarian. His regime of work was punishing: he got up at 4 am, did three hours of work and then took a freezing bath in preparation for the day's labours.

Cripps intended to pursue a financial policy very different from that of his predecessor Dalton. The latter had supposed that the main danger to be avoided was unemployment and had therefore expanded the economy, but in ways that brought in imports in excess of Britain's ability to pay for them. Cripps was determined to make Britain self-reliant by enhancing production and reducing consumption. Resources and manpower were directed towards the export trades. In 1948 exports were 25 per cent above the total for the previous year and the output of the steel industry reached an all-time record. Especially encouraging were the figures for exports to North America, where an economic boom sucked in imports from Britain. By the second half of the year, Britain even enjoyed a small surplus of exports over imports, though trade with the dollar area did not yet balance. For the time being, Britain derived considerable help from the European Recovery Programme (Marshall Aid), financed by the USA, but the roots of recovery were indigenous. Control of consumption was achieved by continuing rationing of food, clothing, petrol and other commodities. There was a great deal of grumbling, particularly among middle-class people, but it seems that the working classes accepted the restrictions as fair and as guaranteeing a higher standard of nutrition than their forefathers had ever known. The necessity of rationing seemed to be demonstrated when sweets were taken off the ration in 1949. There were not enough to meet the pent-up demand and rationing had hastily to be re-imposed.

If Cripps' policy was to work, it was important to keep prices down by means of wage restraint. The trade unions were uneasy about a policy which ran counter to their tradition of collective bargaining with

Exports recover 1948

Britain aided by Marshall Plan

employers, but they were persuaded to vote for a wage freeze in March 1948. Private firms were induced to impose similar curbs on increases in dividends from shares. Backed by powerful right-wing union leaders, who urged the workers to back 'their' Labour government, the freeze lasted till the autumn of 1950. There were unofficial strikes in the London docks in 1948 and 1949, when the government had to proclaim a state of emergency and used troops to unload ships, but despite the wage freeze, these years were remarkable for industrial peace. Britain experienced nothing like the industrial unrest that broke out in France and Italy, and whereas in 1918-23 178 million working days had been lost to strikes, in 1945-50 the total lost was only 9 million.

Wage freeze 1948-50

In 1948 Cripps was immensely successful, but in 1949 things began to go wrong. The Chancellor fell ill and in July had to retire to a sanatorium in Zurich. The business boom in the USA ended and Britain's dollar earnings sharply fell. From the spring onwards, Britain's dollar reserves began to drop at an alarming rate. In the foreign currency markets there was speculation against sterling, as the view gained ground that the pound would have to be devalued (that is, the value of the pound in terms of dollars would be lowered). In this new crisis, as in 1947, Attlee offered no lead at all, and with Cripps in Switzerland, the decisive steps were taken by junior members of the government, such as Gaitskell, Wilson and Douglas Jay, who had become convinced that a devaluation of the pound was inevitable. The only alternative seemed to be high interest rates, severe cuts in government spending and consequent industrial stagnation and high unemployment. Gaitskell and his allies won over Cripps and the Cabinet. In mid-September it was announced that the pound, hitherto worth $4.03, would now be exchanged for $2.80.

Pound devalued 1949

Devaluation had eminently satisfactory results. Exports began to flow again, especially to the USA, where they were assisted not only by the devaluation, but also by a recovery of the American economy which became evident in 1950. The chief objective of devaluation had been to stop the drain of the dollar reserves. The outflow immediately ceased and month by month for the rest of 1949 the dollar reserves mounted. The chronic imbalance in Britain's trade with the dollar area was at last corrected and Britain no longer had to rely on Marshall Aid to help it out. The self-sufficiency at which Cripps had aimed had been achieved at last, though not entirely by means that he had foreseen or wanted. In 1950 the economy was buoyant and growing steadily. The British share of world trade in manufactures rose to 25 per cent, as opposed to 21 per cent in 1937, though the improvement owed much to the slower recovery of manufacturing industry in Europe. Cripps' record at the Treasury was a distinguished one. His period of office was finally ended in October 1950, when illness compelled him to yield his post to the rising star Hugh Gaitskell.

Cripps had been too austere and moralistic to concern himself with matters to do with the Labour Party and its electoral strategy. The main party strategist was Herbert Morrison, who recovered from his heart trouble and political setbacks of 1947. He urged his party to pay heed to the floating voters and especially to the middle class, who, in his view, wanted no more experiments in nationalization. The watchword should now be consolidation.

Nation-alization of steel and iron

The Labour party had already run into difficulty over the issue of the nationalization of the iron and steel industry. The consensus within the party that had supported the other measures of nationalization was lacking in the case of iron and steel. The industry had recovered well from the depression of the 1930s and had a respectable record of production and profitability. The workers within the industry showed no great enthusiasm for its nationalization and labour relations were good: the last significant strike had been in 1926. On the other hand, the industry urgently needed investment, since many steel works were out of date and badly sited. It also required reorganization, since the existing structure provided profits for all firms, regardless of efficiency. Steel was consequently more expensive than it should have been, which pushed up general manufacturing costs. For years the issue of the nationalization of the steel industry was debated in the Cabinet and repeatedly postponed. Supporters, such as Dalton and Bevan, tended to see it as a symbol of the government's socialist commitment, an issue which could restore the government's radical energy and momentum. For opponents and doubters, with Morrison foremost among them, abandonment of the measure would symbolize the transition of the government to consolidation and reassure many potential Labour supporters. Finally, it was agreed to press on with nationalization, which passed into law in late 1949, though its operation was delayed until after the election of February 1950. By this stage, the doubters and opponents within the party had closed ranks and the party presented an appearance of unity on the issue.

The long battles over steel made crystal clear the decline of enthusiasm for further nationalization. Nonetheless, a number of candidates for nationalization emerged from the various party policy committees and the party was to go into the general election of 1950 with a 'shopping list' of industries deemed suitable for nationalization: cement, water supply, the meat wholesale trade, sugar refining and insurance. Even among the politicians most of these proposed measures aroused at best tepid enthusiasm. Their advantages to more than tiny groups in the electorate were hard to discern. The disadvantages to the Labour Party soon became clear. A cartoon figure called 'Mr Cube', wielding the sword of free enterprise, became ubiquitous, while the 'men from the Pru' (the powerful Prudential insurance company) and other local agents of the insurance companies became in effect Conservative election agents as they argued on doorsteps against the Labour policy of nationalization.

Labour doubts over national-ization

Despite saddling itself with a programme of nationalization in which its leaders only half-believed and which had minimal electoral appeal, the Labour Party otherwise took the moderate line advocated by Morrison when it faced the electorate in February 1950. The party stressed its achievement of the Welfare State and Cripps' great accomplishment of economic recovery without any sacrifice of full

1950 General Election

Labour
election
victory

employment. It fought a low-key campaign intended to suggest that the party would simply consolidate the successes of 1945-50. Evidently, the campaign was effective, since the large Conservative lead in the opinion polls of late 1949 was overturned and Labour ended up with 13.3 million votes to the Conservative total of 12.5 million. The Labour Party polled more votes in 1950 than in 1945, but it had lost many seats to a resurgent Conservative opposition, which did particularly well in suburban and commuter constituencies in and around London. With 315 seats to 298 for the Conservatives and 9 for the Liberals, the Labour Party still had a small overall majority. Plainly, the party had staged a marked recovery since the crisis of 1947. Even though his austerity was not to everyone's taste, it was due above all to Cripps, who had restored the government's credibility and morale after the crisis of 1947.

3. Labour's Defeat of 1951

In 1950 nearly all of the electorate was polarized between two political parties, Labour and the Conservatives. Most people, 84 per cent of those eligible, voted and almost 90 per cent of the voters cast their vote for one or other of the two big parties. The Liberals made a great effort to prove that they were still a national party by putting up 500 candidates, but succeeded only in demonstrating the opposite by losing 300 deposits and almost bankrupting themselves. Nationalist parties in Wales and Scotland failed to win any seats.

The polarization of the electorate reflected the class division of mid-20th-century Britain. It was never the case that the working class voted solidly for Labour: the evidence suggests that around a third voted Conservative. Equally, Labour was never bereft of middle- and even upper-class supporters. The Cabinet in 1945-51 included members of the upper class such as Dalton and Cripps and well-to-do, public school-educated men such as Attlee and Gaitskell. Nonetheless, the Labour Party was associated primarily with the working class. Its constitution gave the trade unions a mighty voice within the party and the secret of the party's unity and coherence under Attlee was the firm alliance between the leading ministers and the leaders of the most powerful trade unions, such as Deakin of the transport workers and Lawther of the miners, an alliance reinforced by the powerful presence within the Cabinet of Ernest Bevin, previously leader of the Transport Workers. The party depended heavily on the political levy collected by the unions from their members. In addition, nearly a third of Labour MPs were sponsored by the trade unions.

In many places, Labour's rule was unchallengeable: in the mining villages of the north-east, the mill towns of the north-west and in some large cities such as Newcastle or Swansea. The record of Labour in office between 1945 and 1951 consolidated its support. The working classes were well satisfied with their government's main achievements, especially with full employment and much greater protection against the impoverishing effects of old age and ill-health. The statistics produced by medical authorities, especially those concerned with the examination of schoolchildren, demonstrated remarkable improvements in physique. Deficiency diseases such as rickets were becoming much rarer. Mass radiography, quality controls on milk and soon new forms of vaccination on offer through the NHS brought a rapid reduction in the incidence of tuberculosis. In these ways, Labour's rule had brought great benefits to its core supporters. It is true that under Cripps' austere regime, the consumer was not yet king and individual choice was restricted, but it is likely that the working class did not miss what it had never had. After all, it still preferred to enjoy its pleasures *en masse*, whether watching football matches which often attracted crowds of 60,000 to the great stadiums such as Ibrox or Highbury, or betting on the dogs, or spending holidays at Butlin's.

Labour's achievements in office

Labour's rule had also brought great benefits to the middle class. The universal benefits of state pensions and the NHS were available for them too. The grammar schools were attended disproportionately by the children of middle-class homes. State subsidies for the arts produced cultural offerings chiefly of interest to middle-class clienteles. Yet far from feeling grateful to Labour, the middle class was inclined to lament that things had changed for the worse. Many in the middle class had benefited from the emergent consumer society of the inter-war decades, whereas in the post-war years rationing and other controls limited choice. Cars, for example, were hard to obtain and petrol was rationed till 1949. The pre-war boom in housing for the middle class contrasted with the post-1945 emphasis on public housing. The private housing market was stagnant and it was difficult even to repair or improve existing houses because of the system of licences for building materials. There were many complaints too because domestic servants had become unobtainable and unaffordable. Despite these complaints, many members of the middle class were doing quite nicely, as the buoyant demand for public school places and private insurance made clear. Many in the lower ranks of the middle class, however, were genuinely squeezed. The salaries of teachers, bank clerks and minor civil servants had risen little and the recipients had been hit by inflation and the high level of taxation.

Labour loses middle-class support

Middle-class readiness to tolerate restrictions and accept austerity in the interests of social solidarity did not long survive the end of the war. In 1945 Labour had made inroads in suburban and commuter seats, but as early as 1946 Labour leaders began to worry over the desertion of the party by middle-class voters. Many owners of small businesses, such as small builders and shopkeepers, felt threatened by the Labour Party's nationalization programme, which seemed to indicate a general hostility to private enterprise. The Conservatives responded by developing rhetoric about setting the people free. Their gains in the election of 1950 owed much to the redistribution of parliamentary seats that had just taken place, but they drew advantage too from a subtle shift in priorities evident chiefly among the middle class. In 1945 the accepted priority was to grant a measure of security to every citizen and thereby reinforce the social cohesion of the country. In 1950 many people had come to think that individual choice, freedom from state control and a life with more fun were the goals to be aimed at. The *New Statesman* put this point clearly after the election of 1950: 'to be non-political in 1945 meant to be Labourish', but 'to be non-political in 1950 meant to be Toryish'. It seemed that the political wind was no longer behind Labour as it started on its second term of office.

Despite its loss of seats in the election and its tiny minority, the morale and solidarity of the Labour government seemed at first unimpaired. The trade unions, however, were becoming more restive. The policy of wage restraint was overturned at the TUC conference of September 1950. When the National Union of Railwaymen threatened a national strike, Bevan, who was briefly Minister of Labour in 1951, defended the union as it breached the guidelines for wages policy. There was trouble too over the government's use of wartime Order 1305, which aimed to stop strikes by forcing disputes to be settled by a National Arbitration Tribunal under threat of imprisonment for anyone disregarding its provisions. Fearful of the menace of Communism, which the government believed to be behind industrial unrest, the government resorted to a series of prosecutions of striking workers. Bevan was deeply embarrassed by the issue and initiated moves to get rid of the offensive Order.

Relations with trade unions unsettled

Order 1305 used against strikers

Bevan had strong reasons for discontent not only over Order 1305, but also over the way in which he had been passed over as a claimant to major office. When illness forced Cripps' retirement as Chancellor, Attlee appointed to the post over Bevan's head the younger and less experienced Gaitskell. Again, when Bevin had to retire as Foreign Secretary in 1951, Morrison, not Bevan, got the job. Bevan felt deeply humiliated as he continued to languish in minor posts. He was also becoming critical of the government's foreign policy as Britain was sucked into the Korean War on America's side. He thought it better to seek the defeat of Communism in the realm of ideas and social policy than to oppose it by force and he was particularly worried about the implications of the huge rearmament programme which Britain

Bevan worried by British re-armament

agreed to undertake at the behest of the USA. Inevitably, rearmament squeezed domestic spending and the NHS, with its budget close to £400 million in 1950-51, could not be exempt from a review of its finances. The new Chancellor, Gaitskell, was in considerable difficulty as he sought to draw up his budget. Faced with a defence estimate of £1,250 million, a 50 per cent rise, and the need to find an extra £20 million to raise old age pensions, he sought not only to peg the total NHS budget, but also to raise money by imposing charges for dentures and spectacles. Bevan spoke out strongly against any breach of the principle that the health service should be free and demanded that the defence budget be cut instead. Gaitskell would not budge. The argument became extremely bitter and both principals threatened resignation. At this juncture, Attlee became ill and retired to hospital, but in any case he had no suggestions for resolving the dispute. Within the Cabinet, Bevan was isolated, except for the support of Harold

Resignation
of Harold
Wilson and
Nye Bevan

Wilson. Late in April 1951, Bevan and Wilson resigned. Bevan did his cause no good by his intemperate personal attacks on Gaitskell and his ravings about what he called 'my health service'.

The bitter dispute between Bevan and Gaitskell proved to be the curtain-raiser for a long series of disputes which tore the Labour Party apart during the remainder of the 1950s. The immediate impact seems to have been less damaging, though the quarrel may have helped to sap Attlee's will to carry on and so contributed to his decision to call another election for October 1951. By then the ageing Prime Minister, well into his sixties and continuously in high office since 1940, was wilting, as were other senior members of his team, already depleted by Bevin's death and Cripps' retirement because of ill health. The Korean War was dragging on, without any prospect of an early conclusion. There were serious problems in the Middle East. Yet another balance of payments crisis occurred, as the cost of imports soared and exports

Strains on
the economy
1951

lagged. The enormous rearmament programme was imposing great strains on the economy. Taxes had been put up, food rations had to be reduced and the TUC had to be asked for wage restraint in an attempt to curb inflation. In view of all these problems, the government might have done better to carry on and wait for things to improve, but it seems that Attlee had had enough. The wish of the King to have the election out of the way before he began a tour of Africa finally determined the Prime Minister to appeal to the electorate once more.

General Election called 1951

The Conservatives began the election campaign in the lead. They believed that if only they could avoid alarming the voters, the rightward drift of opinion would bring them victory. The Liberals were able to finance only a little more than a hundred candidates, which meant that in the remaining seats their voters had to choose between the Labour and Conservative candidates. In order to win, the Conservatives had to attract a disproportionate number of these voters. The clear importance in the Conservative party of moderates such as RAB Butler and Harold Macmillan reassured electors that the most important achievements of Labour would be maintained under a Conservative government. The Conservatives promised to address the most conspicuous failing of the Labour government, the continued shortage of houses. Cripps' stress on exports and Gaitskell's commitment to a huge rearmament programme had limited Labour's achievement in this area, but the Conservatives promised to build 300,000 houses a year. Labour campaigned mainly on its record, though it made attempts to arouse fears that the Conservatives might dismantle the Welfare State, allow unemployment to return, or pursue an aggressive foreign policy under Churchill, who was sometimes portrayed as a warmonger.

When the votes were counted, it was found that on another very high turnout Labour had won the most votes, only a few less than 14 million, a higher total than any party was to achieve in the remaining elections of the 20th century and nearly 250,000 more than the Conservatives. In terms of seats, however, the Conservatives were the winners, with 26 more seats than Labour and an overall majority of 15. Labour had lost more ground in the suburban and commuter constituencies of south-east England, but its hold on the urban north

Conservative electoral victory

remained as strong as ever and in Wales it actually increased its dominance.

Labour had lost an election, but it had won an argument. The politicians in power in the 1930s were for the next few decades cast as the 'guilty men', guilty not only of appeasing Hitler, but guilty too for letting down the working men of the country by permitting unemployment and providing inadequate security against life's misfortunes. It was the measure of Labour's achievement that the Conservatives could win an election only by stealing most of Labour's clothes.

X

THE LABOUR PARTY AND THE EMPIRE

1. The British Empire during the Second World War

IN 1943 Winston Churchill pointed out that in 1940 the peoples of the Empire had a good opportunity to throw off the British yoke and make terms with Britain's enemies. He continued:

> But what happened? It was proved that the bonds which unite us, though supple and elastic, are stronger than the tensest steel ... In that dark, terrific, and also glorious hour we received from all parts of His Majesty's Dominions, from the greatest to the smallest, from the strongest and from the weakest... the assurance that we would all go down or come through together. You will forgive me if on this occasion... I rejoice in the soundness of our institutions and proclaim my faith in our destiny.

Churchill's pride was understandable. Of the self-governing Dominions, which did not have to follow Britain's lead in foreign policy, all but Ireland joined in the war against Germany, Italy and Japan. Even in Ireland, which remained neutral, 43,000 men volunteered for the British armed forces. From the Empire as a whole, Britain was able to draw on the services of five million men, not far short of the number provided by Britain itself. Many of these troops were employed mainly in defending their own parts of the Empire. All but a tenth of the 2.5 million Indians under arms were used in India itself. After the Japanese War began, most of the men from Australia and New Zealand were employed in the Pacific theatre, usually under American direction. Yet the Empire made a valuable contribution to the survival of Britain. Canadian pilots helped to win the Battle of Britain, Canadian seamen played an indispensable role in the Battle of the Atlantic and Australian and Indian forces were vital in the war in North Africa. The Empire Day slogan for 1941 was 'One King, One Flag, One Fleet, One Empire'. It did not seem too far from the reality.

Yet the war undoubtedly imposed great strains on the Empire. In a large part of the Far East the outposts of the Empire collapsed before the Japanese onslaught. The war ended with the British back in control, thanks largely to American power, but British power in the region could never seem unchallengeable again. Japanese radio stations had spread propaganda calling for an Asia under the control of Asians and the message had found some willing listeners in British India and elsewhere, though many certainly reflected that if Asian rule meant Japanese rule, they wanted nothing to do with it.

Collapse of British Far Eastern power

In the Middle East war did not bring the collapse of British control, but the great build-up of Imperial forces in the region was much resented. The loyalty of Egypt, which had perforce to be the main British base, was always in doubt. The collaborationist royal government was kept in power largely by British armed might. Had Rommel invaded the Nile Valley, he could well have been welcomed as a liberator. In Iraq too the British kept control by indirect means, through the good offices of the pro-British Prime Minister Nuri as-Said. In 1941 Nuri was overthrown in a coup led by four nationalist generals, of whom the leader was Rashid Ali al-Gaylari. They wished to replace the limited self-rule granted under a treaty of 1932, which had been imposed by Britain, with full independence. They were in touch with the Germans, who provided limited military assistance. Invoking a mutual defence treaty, the British landed Indian troops at Basra and used air power to reverse the effects of the coup. They then occupied the country until 1947. The threat to Britain in Iraq had been encouraged by the war with Germany. No such stimulus was necessary to provoke difficulties in

Nationalist coup in Iraq threatens British interests

Palestine, where there was more or less constant conflict between Arabs and Jews and a recurrent danger of the two communities turning on the British, who tried to hold the ring.

Tensions in Palestinian Mandate

Outside the Far and Middle East the war had unsettling effects too. The war increased the demand for tropical products. Colonial industries were encouraged and colonial societies became more mobile and industrialized. The traditional authorities on whom the British usually relied became less powerful and an educated and politically informed and vocal middle class began to emerge. Concessions made during the war both recognized and further stimulated these developments. Regional councils were created in Northern Rhodesia (now Zambia) and changes were made in Nigeria and the Gold Coast (now Ghana) which gave Africans more say in the governments. Growing political consciousness in Africa produced organizations such as the Kikuyu Central Association in Kenya, proscribed because it was thought to be scheming with the Italians in East Africa, the Nyasaland (now Malawi) National Congress and the National Council of Nigeria. All these developments occurred before the end of the war. Troops returning from overseas with their ideas enlarged and intellectuals coming back from Europe and America after the war were likely to wish to accelerate trends already visible towards greater African participation in the government of African countries.

Movements towards African independence

Britain had won the war thanks to its alliances with the USA and the USSR. Yet neither of these countries was sympathetic to what they regarded as out-dated and morally suspect imperialism. It can be argued that both practised a kind of imperialism, but that did not make them any less ready to point out Britain's sins and sometimes to try to correct them. In order to gain Roosevelt's support in the war, Churchill had been compelled to agree to the Atlantic Charter which proclaimed 'the rights of all peoples to choose the form of government under which they will live'. He then had to spend the rest of the war fending off American suggestions that Hong Kong

Atlantic Charter confirms rights of people to governments of their choice should be handed back to China as a gesture of goodwill, or that henceforth all British colonies should be held in trust from the United Nations. Churchill declared that he had not become Prime Minister in order to preside over the liquidation of the British Empire and would not consent to

> Forty or fifty nations thrusting interfering fingers into the life's existence of the British Empire... After we have done our best to fight the war... I will have no suggestion that the British Empire is to be put into the dock and examined by everybody to see whether it is up to standard.

The USA was to prove less dangerous to the British Empire than Churchill had feared. Putting pressure on Britain to dismantle its Empire became a much less important American interest than limiting the expansion of Communism and the power of Soviet Russia and Communist China. In this more vital objective the British Empire could even be useful. The Americans no longer pressed for the hand-over to China of Hong Kong after 1949. In preserving Malaya as part of the Empire, the British did the valuable job of defeating a Communist insurgency. Communism also proved less of a threat than seemed likely after its triumph in China, partly because movements which adopted the Communist ideology brought on themselves American as well as British hostility.

It may be that the international climate of opinion hostile to empires was most important through its effects on the views of those who ran the British Empire. They realized that the Empire was in effect on probation and had to do more than in the past for the peoples within it. In 1940 a bill was introduced into Parliament to give more generous grants to colonies for their 'development and welfare'. Little came of it, but much more was to be done under another Colonial and Welfare Act of 1945. There was constitutional progress too. In 1943 the Colonial Secretary said that the

International opinion hostile to empires

Colonial and Welfare Act 1945

government was 'pledged to guide colonial people along the road to self-government within the British Empire'. Accordingly, Malta and Ceylon (Sri Lanka) were promised self-government and more liberal constitutions were sanctioned in parts of the West Indies.

Self-government promised to Malta and Ceylon

The Second World War did most to undermine the Empire by eroding the economic basis of British power. Such damage as the loss of 11.5 million tons of shipping, the destruction of about 10 per cent of pre-war national wealth and the liquidation of capital assets abroad worth far more than £1 billion could not be repaired rapidly. Britain had come out of the war as the world's largest debtor nation and its financial weakness gave the USA leverage over its policies. In these circumstances, there had to be a scaling down of British commitments. The defence of distant Dominions such as Australia and New Zealand was in effect entrusted to the USA. It was also evident to the Labour government which took office in 1945 that British rule in the Indian sub-continent would have to be abandoned.

Economic weakness undermines Empire

2. The End of the Indian Raj

British India had always been a political patchwork. Only a little more than half of the land mass was directly ruled by Britain. The rest was a mosaic of princely states, some small, some enormous, governed by hereditary rulers who were limited by their various treaties with the British and were supervised by British officials. If the British were to leave India, there would have to be a substitute for British authority as the basis of the country's unity. Accordingly, the Government of India Act of 1935 aimed to create a political framework for the whole of India. The Act envisaged a federal state, on the lines of Canada or Australia, within which the princely states could have maintained a degree of autonomy. These provisions of the Act were to take effect once a majority of princes had joined the proposed federation.

Government of India Act, 1935

Meanwhile, the reforms affecting the provinces went ahead. They became effectively autonomous. They became much more democratic:

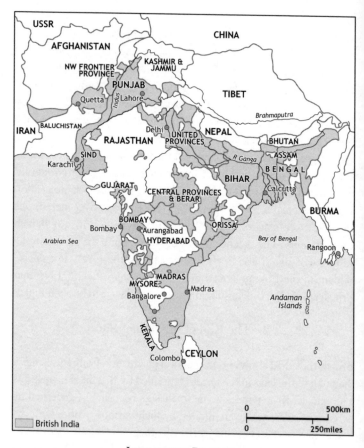

INDIA BEFORE PARTITION

the total electorate was increased to about 35 million (about one out of every six adults). The provincial assemblies were also reorganised so that elected Indian representatives could gain majorities and form governments. Though Nehru described the Act as 'a new charter of slavery', the Congress Party did contest the elections held in 1937 and elected candidates proceeded to take their seats. The Congress Party found itself in control of seven of the eleven provinces. The Party's

Provincial assemblies reorganized

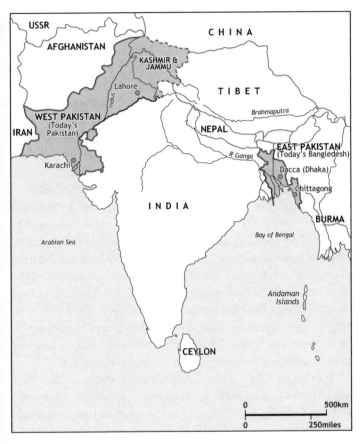

INDIA AFTER PARTITION

high command issued orders to the provincial ministries, but the arrangements helped to entrench the provinces as key foci of Indian political life. They were to play a key role in the states which succeeded British rule.

The most difficult problem raised by the issue of Indian independence had to do with India's diverse religious communities. The majority of the people of the sub-continent were Hindus, but

Tensions between Muslim and Hindu populations

191

there was a very large Muslim minority. The two religions had very different conceptions of God: austere Muslim monotheism, which banned images of Allah, was far removed from Hindu acceptance of large numbers of deities and the reverence shown to their images, viewed by Muslims as idols. Muslims and Hindus were very much communities apart, with different social customs and very little intermarriage. There was a large concentration of Muslims in the north-west, but the map of religious allegiance cut across provincial boundaries. In particular, two provinces were religiously divided.

Religious divisions in Bengal and Punjab
Largely Hindu in the west, Bengal had large numbers of Muslims in its eastern half. Even more divided was the Punjab, with a majority of Muslims towards the west and a Hindu majority to the east. The additional complicating factor here was the presence of yet another religious community, the Sikhs, who rejected both the Muslim practice of circumcision and the Hindu emphasis on caste. The constitution of 1935 dealt with the religious problem at the local level by establishing a complex system of separate electorates for different religious communities in order to ensure that all were represented. At the centre, it was expected that a federal system would go a long way towards satisfying the interests of the various communities.

The Congress Party aimed to establish a secular state in which there would be no official religion. Therefore they saw no reason why Indians of all religions should not join their party and why they should not speak for everyone. Inevitably, though, most members of the Congress Party would be Hindus. Not all Muslims were prepared to trust that their community would be fairly treated by a Hindu majority

Muslim distrust of Congress Party
and they began to demand safeguards. In 1906 the Muslim League was founded in order to formulate and advance the Muslim point of view, though it lacked mass support until the late 1930s. The League was at first inclined to think that the federal constitution of 1935 might give it what it required by way of safeguards, but it soon changed its mind. The Congress Party rejected the League's demands for power-sharing at the provincial level and the pressure applied to the princes

by Congress to popularize their regimes raised the spectre of a Congress majority in a future all-Indian assembly. Both the princes and the Muslim League turned against the federal constitution which they had once welcomed. From 1936 the leader of the Muslim League was Muhammad Ali Jinnah, a man of intimidating determination and an able political tactician. He raised the cry of 'Islam in danger' and it proved so effective that the League won the mass support which it had hitherto lacked. It was soon clear that the federal constitution of 1935 was doomed.

Muhammad Ali Jinnah

When the Second World War started, the Viceroy simply informed Indians that they were at war. The Congress Party was outraged and its ministers resigned from the provincial governments, allowing the British to impose direct rule and wartime restrictions. The Muslim League promptly declared a Day of Deliverance from the oppression of what Jinnah called the 'Congress Raj'. Jinnah later said, 'The war which nobody welcomed proved to be a blessing in disguise.' The League was finally established as the spokesman for the majority of Muslims and it acquired an objective, defined in the Lahore Resolution of 1940. Based on the premise that the Muslims of India effectively constituted a nation, the Resolution called for a constitution allowing areas where Muslims were in a numerical majority, such as the northwest and east, to constitute independent states. Much was left for the future to determine, such as the geographical extent of the projected states and whether the states should be combined in a federation or not. Should a federation come into existence, a new name had already been coined by a small group of Muslim intellectuals at Cambridge. Their neologism was 'Pakistan', formed from the initial letters of Punjab, Afghans (meaning the Pathans), Kashmir and Sind together with 'stan', the Persian suffix meaning 'country'. The Resolution gave Muslims a goal to rally round, which greatly aided them in the forthcoming negotiations with Britain and struggles with Congress.

Lahore Resolution 1940

Origin of the name Pakistan

Shaken by the successes of the Japanese in Malaya, Singapore and Burma, and anxious to shore up their support in India, the British

Stafford
Cripps in
India

took a significant initiative in 1942. At the instance of Clement Attlee, then deputy Prime Minister, Sir Stafford Cripps was sent on a mission to India. Cripps was known to be sympathetic to Indian independence and he made a clear offer of Dominion status as soon as the war was over. Effectively, the Indians were being offered independence. The offer did not impress Indian leaders, since they already assumed that independence would follow the war. The debate had moved on to the issue of what exactly would be independent. Congress still championed the notion of a single, indivisible Indian nation of which it claimed to be the spokesman. Cripps, however, seemed inclined to offer concessions to the Muslims and princes.

Gandhi's
'Quit India'
Campaign

The British had hoped for reconciliation with India's leaders, but instead there came confrontation. Gandhi hated all wars including the one between Britain and Japan. He argued that only immediate British withdrawal and a declaration of Indian neutrality could save India from Japanese attack. He therefore proposed a fresh non-violent challenge to British rule, his 'Quit India' campaign. The Viceroy's government at once pounced on Gandhi and other Congress leaders and imprisoned them. Strikes and boycotts, sabotage of telegraph and railway lines, explosions at police and railway stations ensued in what Viceroy Linlithgow reckoned the most serious revolt since the Mutiny. It was leaderless, however, and in wartime the government had massive force at its disposal. There was never any prospect, then, that British rule might be overthrown. Yet it was obvious to many in Britain that if such application of force was necessary to uphold British rule in India, then the writing really was on the wall. In peacetime, Britain would not have such force at its disposal and in any case would not dare to use it given the likely reaction of international and especially American opinion.

Churchill's defeat in the general election of 1945 meant the fall from office of a man who had a romantic attachment to Britain's Indian Empire and was extremely loath to dismantle it. Attlee, by contrast, had no doubt that the British had to quit India. He had been involved with Indian affairs since the discussions of the late 1920s and was to exert a powerful influence at every stage of the prolonged discussions about India in the first two years of his administration.

At the end of the war, there seemed to be a total impasse as every initiative foundered on the intransigence of the spokesmen for Congress and the Muslim League. New elections called in 1946 simply confirmed the polarization of Indian opinion. A British Cabinet mission was therefore sent to India with the aim of finding a solution, but its plan for a loose all-India federation with complex safeguards for religious minorities foundered when it came to working out the details and deciding on an interim government. Recriminations led to a call from the League to the 'Muslim nation' to engage in direct action. The Muslim League ministry in Calcutta responded by calling a public holiday for everyone, including the police. Muslims took the opportunity to loot and burn Hindu shops. Murder was soon added to the crimes committed and the Hindus started to fight back. Over three days the Calcutta Killings claimed about four thousand lives. The inter-communal riots then spread to East Bengal and Bihar. A horrified Nehru declared that 'a madness has seized the people'. Gandhi toured the devastated communities to preach reconciliation.

Muslims burn and loot Hindu shops August 1946

With law and order collapsing in many places and with the police unreliable where communities were divided, the British government resolved on an early evacuation of British troops. Yet it was also determined not to allow India to dissolve into chaos, but to hand over power to Indian authorities. Attlee decided to sack Viceroy Wavell, who seemed to have lost all hope of a constructive outcome, and to appoint instead Louis Mountbatten. Mountbatten had a number of advantages. As cousin of the King-Emperor George VI, he had a standing superior to that of any politician. He had no preconceptions about India and was not associated with any particular group or solution. His huge ego gave him a confidence which proved useful in the job he had to do and his great charm was also a helpful quality.

Louis Mountbatten appointed Viceroy

Attlee also believed that a deadline would help to concentrate minds and in February 1947, he announced that British forces would leave no later than June 1st 1948.

Mountbatten was left in total charge of negotiations with Congress, the League and the Sikhs. Things proceeded at a smart pace and by June Mountbatten could announce that Congress and the League had agreed that power should be transferred to two successor states, India and Pakistan, which would each acquire Dominion status. The two most divided provinces, Bengal and the Punjab, were to be partitioned along sectarian lines. The princely states were to be urged to join one of the successor states. The end of the Raj was advanced to 15 August 1947. Nehru had got on extremely well with Mountbatten, and even better with the latter's wife, Edwina. The Viceroy was present in Delhi as Nehru gave an oration which could have been modelled on those of Churchill.

The end of
the Raj
August 1947

> Long years ago we made a tryst with destiny, and now the time comes when we shall redeem our pledge, not wholly or in full measure but very substantially. At the stroke of the midnight hour, when the world sleeps, India will awake to life and freedom. A moment comes, which comes but rarely in history, when we step out from the old to the new, when an age ends, and when the soul of a nation, long suppressed, finds utterance. It is fitting that at this solemn moment we take the pledge of dedication to the service of India and her people and to the still larger cause of humanity.

The Raj seemed to end, at governmental level, in an atmosphere of goodwill. Both India and Pakistan joined the Commonwealth, which had to be modified somewhat, since both had become republics. The Labour Party preened itself on its successful resolution of the difficult problems which the decolonization of India entailed. Yet it was not exactly the case that everyone lived happily ever after. The creation of

The creation
of India and
Pakistan

the new states meant the partition of two great historic provinces, Bengal and the Punjab. The task of dissecting the former was accomplished with relative ease, though many Muslims and Hindus found themselves on the wrong side of the new frontier and there were many refugees in both directions. Partition was unfortunate too in its economic results. East Bengal was left as an impoverished 'rural slum', split from the wealthier and more industrialised West Bengal, which included Calcutta. The problems of the Punjab were very much greater, partly because the Sikhs had to be accommodated as well as the Hindus and Muslims. Forcible expulsions and migration took place on an enormous scale: perhaps ten million people were involved in this, the greatest exodus in recorded history. There was violence too on a gigantic scale. The troops who were supposed to keep the situation under control themselves took sides in the conflict. The number of dead has never been computed, but half a million people or more may have perished. Delhi itself was affected, as the Hindus sought to expel the Muslims. In October Gandhi arrived in the capital to attempt reconciliation. When India and Pakistan quarrelled over the division of assets inherited from the British, he went on hunger strike until they resolved the dispute. A few days after the end of his successful fast, on 30 January 1948, as he went to a prayer meeting, he was shot three times in the chest by a Hindu fanatic, Nathuram Godse. The strife between India's communities had claimed its most illustrious victim. At the funeral Nehru spoke: 'Friends and Comrades, the light has gone out of our lives, and there is darkness everywhere ... Our beloved leader, Bapu ... the Father of the Nation, is no more.'

The inter-communal violence was the most terrible result of Partition, but it brought other misfortunes to the sub-continent too. One of the most significant was the apparently permanent enmity between Pakistan and India. At Partition, the princely states were left to make their own decisions between accession to India or Pakistan. Both states were determined to gain control of Kashmir. The 'K' in

Partition of Bengal and Punjab

Refugees and forcible expulsions

Gandhi assassinated January 1948

Dispute over Kashmir

Pakistan stands for Kashmir and the majority of the inhabitants are Muslim. The Maharaja, however, was Hindu and Congress had the support of some popular organizations. In the autumn of 1947 undeclared war broke out as Pakistani and Indian forces invaded the country. In 1948 the United Nations brokered a ceasefire and ever

Undeclared war between India and Pakistan

since Indian and Pakistani forces have glowered at each other across a frontier that neither side recognizes as final. Sixty years after independence the dispute continues to poison relations between the two heirs of the Raj and to make India a target for *jihad* (Muslim holy war).

The Pakistan which emerged at Partition did not prove a satisfactory state. East Bengal was separated from the rest of the country by more than a thousand miles of Indian territory and its special interests tended to be ignored by the governments based in the

East Bengal becomes Bangladesh 1971

west. After a quarter of a century of tensions, East Bengal finally became independent as Bangladesh.

The settlement which the British worked out as they left India left the successor states and their peoples enormous problems, but it is probably unrealistic to suppose that the greatest of them, the division between the Muslim and Hindu communities, with all its fateful consequences, could have been avoided. On the whole, the praise usually accorded to Attlee's government for its handling of the difficult situation is probably justified. Things could so easily have been much worse, as the stories of post-colonial Indo-China or Zaire, or post-Communist Yugoslavia was to suggest.

At the same time that they were dealing with the problem of India, the Labour government was also in the process of granting

Sri Lankan Independence

independence elsewhere in southern Asia. Sri Lankan independence was not controversial and was carried through in 1948. Britain was not 'scuttling' (Churchill's description) from Asia altogether. Troubles in the 1930s had made it clear that Burma too could not easily be preserved as a colony. It gained its independence in 1948.

3. The Problem of Palestine

At the official level at least, Britain's exit from the Indian sub-continent was reasonably dignified. The same cannot be said of its surrender of its responsibilities in Palestine.

The situation in Palestine facing the Attlee government when it took office in 1945 was fraught with difficulty. An Arab revolt in 1936-9 had led to a round table conference, at which the British government consulted with the two hostile communities of the Jews and the Arabs, who put forward totally incompatible demands. The Jews, most of them recent immigrants who had often escaped from persecution in Europe, demanded unlimited immigration of co-religionists, the unrestricted right to purchase land and a homeland of their own, in accordance with the Balfour Declaration of 1917. The Arabs did not recognize the Balfour Declaration as having any binding force. They saw Palestine as an Arab land and refused to recognise the Jews as a separate community with special rights. They were particularly concerned to prevent more Jewish immigration and Jewish acquisition of additional land.

Much to the frustration of the British, no agreement could be reached between the Jews and the Arabs. Arab goodwill was extremely important to the British, who could not afford to alienate the Egyptians, whose support was vital if Britain's hold on the Suez Canal was to be secure. Britain also needed to keep states such as Iraq and Saudi Arabia friendly, in view of their increasing importance as oil producers. It was therefore essential to rein back Jewish ambitions. Hence, the British insisted in a White Paper of 1939 that Jewish immigration should be limited to 75,000 over the next five years. The Zionists were adamant that this limit was grossly inadequate. During the war years, they tried to bring immigrants in illegally, while the British were determined to enforce the limit. On occasion, the British kept out even people with a strong humanitarian case as refugees from the extermination policies pursued by the Nazis in Europe. Some of

White Paper on Jewish immigration 1939

the Jews resorted to terrorist activity. In 1944 Lord Moyne, the British Minister Resident, was murdered by the Stern Gang.

Assassination of Lord Moyne 1944

When the Labour Party formed its government in 1945, it was widely believed that Britain's policy would become much more favourable to the Jews. There were influential Jewish MPs in the government and important ministers such as Dalton and Morrison were friendly to the Jewish cause. The revelations about the Nazi extermination camps made it hard to deny that the Jews needed a homeland of their own. Britain was also put under pressure to make concessions to the Jews by President Truman, who was himself pushed by the powerful Jewish lobby within the Democratic party. Yet in the end, British policy did not alter significantly. Usually, the Foreign Secretary, Ernest Bevin, is blamed for the lack of change. Though not anti-semitic, Bevin was notably unsympathetic to the Zionist cause and wholly failed to understand the passion behind it. It was unfortunate that British policy was not presented by a more emollient personality. Bevin did not, however, make policy on his own. Attlee consistently supported his Foreign Secretary's policy, as did the powerful Palestine Committee. British statesmen could all see the irresponsibility of Jewish demands, backed by America, for unrestricted Jewish immigration into Palestine. As holder of the Mandate for the area, Britain had to consider the repercussions of Jewish demands on law and order within Palestine and on the stability of the whole Middle East. It also could not afford to forget that it needed Arab goodwill much more than it needed Jewish goodwill.

Appeals for a Jewish homeland

Jewish terrorism in Palestine

Many of the Jews believed that the only way of forcing Britain to accept their point of view was by intensifying their campaign of terrorism. They kidnapped British officials and sabotaged the infrastructure of Palestine by attacking the railways and bridges. Despairing of a political solution, the British resorted to military repression. A curfew was imposed on the population and thousands of arrests were made. The climax of this phase of the crisis was the

BOMBING OF THE KING DAVID HOTEL, JULY 1946
Courtesy of the Imperial War Museum

blowing up of the King David Hotel in July 1946 by a terrorist organization called the Irgun, led by Menachem Begin. The Hotel was chosen because the British military command had its base in the south wing. Ninety-one people were killed, among them British, Arabs and Jews.

Bombing of the King David Hotel July 1946

By 1947 the situation had become intolerable. Attempts to resolve the issues at a conference were boycotted by the Jews and the Palestinian Arabs. Yet things could not go on as they were. British opinion was inflamed by the deaths of British soldiers and the Palestine commitment became increasingly unpopular. Great numbers of troops were tied down at a cost which Britain could no longer afford. The issue caused quarrels between Britain and America at a time when American help in Europe was desperately needed. The necessity of bases in Palestine was questionable, even if, as seemed possible at the time, Britain had to withdraw from the Canal Zone. In February, therefore, the whole matter was referred to the United Nations, which set up a committee to examine it.

The UN committee reported in favour of a partition of Palestine into Jewish and Arab states. To this 'solution' Bevin could see every kind of objection. A huge military presence would be needed to oversee a partition which could not be amicable. Every Arab country would be outraged. In September 1947 the British Cabinet decided that Britain would have to surrender its responsibilities under the Mandate and pull out its troops in 1948. The UN General Assembly duly endorsed partition and the inevitable civil war followed between the Arab Liberation Army and the Zionist militants. When an armistice was patched up by the UN in early 1949, a Jewish state had emerged, which Britain proceeded to recognize. The Palestinian Arab areas of the coastal strip round Gaza and the West Bank of the Jordan were loosely attached to the Arab Kingdom of Jordan, which the British had set up to govern all the areas of their Mandate east of the Jordan River. The British maintained bases in Jordan under a treaty with the state: Britain had no intention of abandoning the area altogether.

Britain surrenders Mandate

UN endorses partition

In Palestine, unlike in India, Britain had not handed over power to an alternative authority. It had abdicated its responsibilities and left the rival communities to fight it out. A more humiliating outcome can hardly be imagined. Yet it is impossible to see how an over-stretched British government could have done better. More than sixty years later, the problem of Palestine continues to defy all efforts to resolve it.

4. The Dependent Empire

In Palestine and the Indian sub-continent the post-war Labour government ended direct British involvement, but it had no intention of dismembering the Empire entirely. The Fabian Colonial Research Bureau had influence within the party and one of its members, Arthur Creech Jones, became Colonial Secretary. He believed that self-government could be responsibly given to colonies only when economic prosperity had been achieved, since prosperity was essential to political stability. Creech Jones followed up the Colonial Development and Welfare Act of 1945 by founding the Colonial Development Corporation, which energetically pursued grand economic schemes. There were some notable failures, like the scheme to grow ground nuts in Tanganyika, where neither rainfall nor soil had been studied to make sure that the nuts would actually grow. Yet a significant stimulus was given to the economic growth of the colonies of East and West Africa. *(Colonial Development Corporation)*

Altruism was a powerful force in the post-war Colonial Office, but money had to be obtained from a hard-pressed Treasury, which expected to see a return on its outlay. One of Britain's greatest problems in the post-war period was to earn enough dollars to finance its purchases from the USA. The colonies were all members of the Sterling Area, which meant that their dollar earnings went into the common pool and became available for Britain to use. Hence, the Treasury was keen that colonies should produce dollar-earning products, or alternatively products which could replace those bought in dollars, like East African vegetable oils or Southern Rhodesian tobacco. It followed that economic development in the colonies tended to reflect British needs and was not geared to creating balanced economies which might better suit the colonies when they did become self-governing. Creech Jones also established the Overseas Food Corporation, designed to buy in bulk from the colonies such staple crops as cocoa, tobacco and cotton. It helped to give the colonies an *(Overseas Food Corporation)* assured market, but also was of advantage to Britain by keeping prices below world levels.

The most valuable dependency of all was Malaya. There the British were faced with Communist terrorism, stemming from the alienation of the strong Chinese community. A state of emergency was imposed from June 1948 and for five years British troops fought the insurgents. The country provided more than half of the US imports of rubber and most of its tin and was therefore a big dollar-earner for the Sterling Area. There was no question of withdrawing from so valuable a colony, or of American pressure on Britain to do so.

State of emergency in Malaya 1948

Creech Jones was concerned not only with the economic development of the colonies, but also planning and controlling their political evolution. He did not believe, as pre-war colonial ministers had mostly believed, that Africans would not be ready for self-government for many decades. If they might be ready in the near future, then it was important to prepare for it. Policy makers hoped to shape colonial independence movements, instead of being overwhelmed by them, as had occurred in India. In May 1947 the Cohen Report envisaged that many of the colonies would be self-governing within a generation. It advised that Britain should prepare by establishing new middle-class elites and systems of local government no longer dependent on traditional tribal authorities. The aim was an orderly transfer of power to stable, pro-British governments.

The Cohen Report

The approach of the post-war Colonial Office was to be implemented most successfully in West Africa, where there were no significant numbers of white settlers to complicate the situation. By 1950 the new constitution for the Gold Coast (Ghana) guaranteed an African majority in the decision-making bodies, while the constitution of 1951 for Nigeria attempted to create a federal structure to accommodate the very different societies of the south and north of the country. Development was not wholly smooth: after disturbances in Accra, the Gold Coast political leader was for a time imprisoned. Yet it

New Constitutions in Gold Coast and Nigeria

looked as though independence would come before long and without the disturbances that had characterized the end of the Indian Raj.

Elsewhere, the omens were less good. The Colonial Office took up the idea of federations as a way of promoting stability. In the Far East the colonies round the South China Sea appeared too small and weak to survive on their own, especially in view of the danger from Communism in the area. A federation of Singapore, Malaya and the British-held parts of Borneo looked a promising way round the difficulties. In South Africa the threat might come from an expansionist South Africa, dominated since the election of 1948 by the strongly anti-British, militantly Afrikaner government of Dr DF Malan's National Party. There was a conference at Victoria Falls in 1949, where the demand for a federation of Northern and Southern Rhodesia and Nyasaland was first effectively voiced. A tempting feature of the arrangement was that Southern Rhodesia (Zimbabwe), with a government dominated by the 200,000 white settlers in the country, could be a force for stability. In fact, the potential power of this white minority made the proposed federation unlikely to get off the ground. The Nyasaland African Congress, led by Dr Hastings Banda, believed that the plan was to 'sacrifice them to please the European settlers of Rhodesia'. Yet another federation was suggested for East Africa, where a white-led Kenya might act as a force for stability.

Nyasaland African Congress

A notable characteristic of Labour's colonial policy was how little criticism it aroused at home. Most of Labour's supporters were not much interested in the Empire in any case and among the public in general, so opinion polls revealed, ignorance about the Empire was profound. According to a poll of 1948, half of the population could not name a single British colony. The leading idea of the period, the concept of trusteeship, was common to those who cared about the Empire in both main political parties. What Labour gave away – chiefly India – was already agreed by most politicians, apart from a few incurable (and usually elderly) romantics like Churchill, to be impossible to keep. It could even be argued that Britain was not really coming down in the world, because the old-fashioned, somewhat offensive-sounding Empire was being replaced by a more modern-sounding Commonwealth.

5. The Commonwealth

Between the wars the term 'British Commonwealth' was applied exclusively to the white Dominions, Canada, Australia, New Zealand and South Africa. After 1945 the Labour government in Britain continued to be closely linked with the white Dominions. Cordial personal relationships between the leading ministers of the various countries helped, but economic ties were still very important. Vital imports came to Britain from the Dominions: meat from Australia, dairy products from New Zealand, wheat and timber from Canada and uranium and gold from South Africa. The Commonwealth provided markets for British manufactures too: in 1950 the Commonwealth took 41.55 per cent of British exports and re-exports. There was also an important defence aspect to the Commonwealth. The issue was central at Commonwealth conferences in 1946 and 1947 and a Commonwealth Defence Committee was set up. In the Korean War of 1950-3 a 'Commonwealth Division' participated, comprising British, Canadian, Australian and New Zealand troops and an Indian ambulance unit. The victory of the Afrikaner nationalists in the South African election of 1948 looked likely to weaken the ties between Britain and South Africa, but anti-Communism was still a common link and Britain continued to rely on the Simonstown naval base.

The period of Attlee's government saw one departure from the Commonwealth, that of Éire. De Valera had already cut virtually all the ties between southern Ireland and the United Kingdom and it made good sense to regularize the situation and recognize Ireland as a republic. Irish wishes were largely met on matters of immigration and trade. Of course, the Irish issue was not dead and buried, since

Common-
wealth
Defence
Committee

the treaty of 1949 recognised the partition of Ireland into north and south, an outcome that was not acceptable to a large minority in the north. Eventually, Irish issues would return to haunt British and Irish politics again.

1949 was also the year when the Commonwealth was enlarged by a new member, in the wake of a decision which proved to be crucial for its future. India had declared itself a republic after independence, but it wished still to remain a member of the Commonwealth. The Foreign Office was anxious that India's request should be favourably received, so that Britain might retain influence on newly independent India and, in particular, keep it from aligning itself with the Communist bloc. Republican India was allowed to be a member of the Commonwealth, accepting the King as Head of the Commonwealth, though not as its own head of state. The road to a politically varied and multi-racial Commonwealth had been opened, though inevitably this development meant the end of the close-knit Commonwealth which had fought in the two world wars. Yet that old Commonwealth was destined to become more attenuated in any case. Its essential glue had been Britain's world-wide power, which had been so gravely weakened. Britain could now only defend itself in Europe by joining a regional defence pact, the North Atlantic Treaty Organization (NATO), in which only the only Dominion with a role was Canada. Britain was anxious to join a South-East Asian pact with Australia and New Zealand, but the USA did not want such a pact to have a colonialist taint and excluded Britain. The USA now called the shots in this area and had its way.

Britain joins NATO 1949

At the end of Labour's period in office, it was already clear that the Commonwealth could never become a vehicle for the projection of British power. If it had been, it would not have endured very long, since too few of its members wanted to perpetuate British power. Instead, it survived as a helpful system of informal contacts, enhancing Britain's influence in some places, though also enhancing the influence of other members on Britain.

VI

BRITISH FOREIGN POLICY
AT THE START OF THE COLD WAR

1. The Disintegration of the Wartime Alliance

THE alliance of Britain, the United States and the Soviet Union which had fought and defeated Hitler's Germany in the Second World War was always an alliance of convenience. At times, on the British side, a certain warmth entered into the relationship between Britain and the USSR. British newspapers were apt to salute the heroism of 'our Russian allies', and Churchill sometimes fancied that he could depend on the personal relationship that he had established with the Soviet dictator. In early 1944 he wrote to Foreign Secretary Eden of 'the new confidence which has grown in our hearts towards Stalin'. Usually, however, he was more realistic. Stalin had no love of the West. He recalled that the Western powers had intervened against the Bolsheviks in the Russian Civil War and that for years they had treated the USSR as a rogue state. He suspected that they had hoped for a war between the USSR and Nazi Germany, in which the two powers would destroy each other. His suspicions kept re-surfacing during the war itself: the delay in opening a second front seemed like a policy to bleed the Soviet Union white as it struggled alone against the Nazis, so that an undamaged West could inherit control of Europe.

The West's love affair with Stalin was a recent and temporary phenomenon too. The USSR had sponsored the Comintern from 1919 onwards, an organization which sought to destabilize Western regimes and establish Communist governments instead. Something was known in the West of the secret police, the labour camps and the bloody purges that were integral to the Stalinist system of control. If many had felt inclined to trust Stalin when he supported popular fronts against Nazism in the later 1930s, he had revealed himself as a shameless and untrustworthy opportunist when he had signed his Pact with Nazi Germany in 1939. During the war, a recurrent nightmare of the West was that he might make a separate peace with Hitler. This fear seemed plausible because there was something unnatural about the wartime alliance of Britain, the USA and the USSR. These allies were united only by a temporary common purpose, the aim of defeating Hitler and the Japanese. It was always likely that once the common purpose was achieved, the alliance would dissolve. What was not so certain was that it would be succeeded by the prolonged state of mutual hostility which we call the Cold War.

Stalin's opportunism breeds distrust

Stalin's main concern, once the war was won, was security. Twice in Stalin's lifetime Russia had been invaded by the Germans and in 1941-2 they had come within a hair's breadth of destroying the state altogether. Perhaps as much as a tenth of the Soviet population had perished in a terrible war. To prevent such an invasion from happening again, Stalin was determined to secure the boundaries conceded under the Nazi-Soviet Pact of 1939, together with a sphere of influence in Eastern Europe, which would afford the USSR protection against any further attack from the West.

Russian war casualties

Churchill appreciated Stalin's need for security. Given the enormous price in blood and treasure paid by the peoples of the Soviet Union, it was hard to deny that they deserved greater security in recompense for their sufferings. Churchill realized too that with the advance of the Red Army into Eastern Europe, Stalin was in a very strong position to determine the destiny of the states he had invaded. In these circumstances, it seemed impossible to do more than limit Stalin's ambitions. This was the point of the 'Percentages Agreement' of October 1944. In a meeting with Stalin in Moscow, Churchill scribbled some proposals on the back of an envelope. Romania was to be 90 per cent a Russian interest, 10 per cent a British one; Greece 90 per cent British, 10 per cent Russian; Bulgaria 75 per cent Russian, 25 per cent British; Hungary and Yugoslavia 50 per cent each. Stalin

'Percentages Agreement'

looked at the list, ticked it and passed it back. The main point, from Churchill's point of view, was to prevent Stalin from intervening in the civil war which was raging in Greece between Communists and royalists and to preserve the eastern Mediterranean as a British sphere of influence: a southern limit to Stalin's sphere of interest had been set. Stalin, presumably, was pleased to receive British acceptance of his position in Eastern Europe in advance of the peace conference which was expected after the war was over.

Russian and British spheres of interest

Churchill also discussed with Stalin the tricky question of Poland. Two sets of men claimed to speak for Poland, a government-in-exile based in London since 1939, and the Lublin Committee, a group hand-picked by the Soviets to take over once Warsaw was liberated. Stalin was determined to secure a government friendly to the Soviet Union, which the London Poles most certainly were not. It was already obvious that Stalin would get his way, since his troops occupied Poland, but Stalin's demands could not so easily be rubber-stamped by Churchill: Britain had originally gone to war over the issue of Poland and its fate was of concern to the British public, whereas that of Nazi ex-allies such as Hungary or Romania was not. The Polish issue was left to what turned out to be the last meeting of the three great leaders in the war against Hitler.

The Polish question

Roosevelt had not been present when Churchill and Stalin made their Percentages Agreement. Desperately ill, he did attend the meeting of the 'Big Three' at Yalta in the Crimea in February 1945. The main point of the meeting, for the Americans, was to secure Stalin's entry into the war against Japan, but given that the Red Army had overrun Poland, it was not possible to ignore the question of the country's future, controversial though it was. Stalin insisted on a government dominated by the Lublin Poles and could not be denied, since the West still wished to continue the wartime alliance. All three powers signed the Declaration on Liberated Europe, whereby the three Allied governments agreed jointly to assist the peoples of any state liberated from Axis control to form representative governments

The Yalta Conference February 1945

Declaration on Liberated Europe

CHURCHILL, ROOSEVELT AND STALIN AT YALTA, FEBRUARY 1945

and hold free elections. Churchill and Roosevelt had to hope that his acceptance of the Declaration meant that Stalin would not insist on converting the countries of eastern Europe into one-party states politically and economically closed to all western influence. Churchill at least feared from the start that he might have 'underwritten a fraudulent prospectus'. So it proved. 'Do not worry,' said Stalin to his Foreign Minister Molotov. 'We can implement it [the Declaration] in our own way later. The heart of the matter is the correlation of forces.' The 'correlation of forces' – Stalin's overwhelming military strength in Poland – gave Churchill little real choice in the matter.

The reasonably cordial atmosphere of the Yalta conference in February is often contrasted with the more quarrelsome mood of the

Potsdam
Conference
July 1945

Potsdam conference in July, 1945. The change is sometimes attributed to the substitution of Harry Truman for Franklin Roosevelt after the latter's death in April. The main difference, however, was that the Americans no longer needed the alliance. They could not, at that stage, prevent a Soviet declaration of war on Japan, but their possession of a tested atomic bomb made a Soviet war against Japan unnecessary and even embarrassing, since they had no intention of giving Stalin large rewards for his help. If the alliance with the USSR was no longer necessary to the USA, the incentive to overlook underlying animosities and differences of interest was much weakened. Stalin's suppression in his sphere of influence in Eastern Europe of what the West regarded as basic freedoms – a choice between several parties in elections, the existence of media not under state control, freedom from arbitrary arrest and the like – began to be held against him. Stalin was held responsible for a division of Europe into two zones, a 'free' zone and a Communist zone. This was the theme of ex-Prime Minister Churchill in a speech given in Fulton, Missouri in 1946, when he spoke of a continent divided by an iron curtain.

The 'Iron
Curtain'

Clement Attlee and his Foreign Secretary Ernest Bevin fully shared Churchill's suspicion of Soviet Russia. Both detested Communism: for years they had fought to exclude it from the Labour Party and trade union movement. As members of the wartime coalition government, both had an exalted conception of Britain's place in the world. 'We regard ourselves as one of the Powers most vital to the peace of the world,' said Bevin in 1947. Both regarded Stalin as a threat to Britain's status and power. Apart from subjugating eastern Europe, Stalin was preventing progress towards a German settlement by insisting on extravagant reparations. Though Stalin did not stir up the large Communist parties in France and Italy, their existence much increased fears that he might try to take over Western Europe as he had already taken over the East. The Soviet Union seemed also to be pursuing the ambitions of the Tsars towards the south. It sought a new agreement with Turkey over the Dardanelles, the Russian entry-

Soviet
ambitions in
the south

COLD WAR CONFRONTATION

point to the Mediterranean. It requested a share of Italy's former colonial empire in North Africa. In 1946 Soviet troops stayed on in Iran beyond the time agreed for their departure.

Interpretation of Soviet actions was not straightforward. Stalin was certainly obsessed with security, but it was not clear whether he was bent on unlimited expansion, as Hitler had been. The British Foreign Office was at first inclined to give him the benefit of the doubt, but the unending stream of Marxist propaganda attacking the Western powers as well as Stalin's actions gradually convinced the policy-makers that they were facing another aggressive dictator. Chamberlain's fatal policy of appeasement was fresh in their memories as an example of what to avoid when dealing with an aggressive ruler. The supposed lessons of the 1930s inclined British and American statesmen to stand up to Stalin. Confrontation short of war between the Soviets and the West was the defining characteristic of the Cold War.

Yet it was not at first certain that Stalin would have to deal with a more or less united West. The Communist leader himself expected that the wartime alliance of Britain and America would prove no more durable than his own alliance with the West. The inability of the capitalist states in the 1930s to agree on any common approach to tackling the economic problems associated with the Great Depression stemmed, in Stalin's view, from the very nature of capitalist states, where most economic activity remained in the hands of privately owned companies. The greed of businessmen ensured that such states could never co-operate for long. In the post-war period Stalin confidently awaited the breakdown of the Anglo-American alliance, which would give him excellent opportunities for widening still further his sphere of influence.

Post-war
Anglo-
American
relations
The differing interests of Britain and the USA had been evident during the war, when the Americans had vetoed any British proposals concerning the war against Japan which seemed to be aimed chiefly at restoring the British Empire rather than at the defeat of Japan. American suspicion of Churchill's efforts to concentrate the Allied military effort in Europe in Italy and Greece stemmed from the belief that he was chiefly aiming to reconstruct a traditional British sphere of influence in the Mediterranean. Empires and spheres of influence were supposed to belong to a discredited past. Once the war was over, it looked as if the Americans would once more retreat into isolation. The number of their troops in Europe was rapidly reduced, from 3.5 million at the end of the war in Europe to 200,000 two years later. The USA retreated also from its wartime promises of co-operation with Britain over the development of atomic energy. The British had played an important role in the original research which had borne fruit in the making of the bomb and were resentful when promises were broken under pressure from Congress and they were excluded from further developments in the field.

There were also disputes between the British and the Americans over economic issues. Lend-Lease, introduced by the USA in 1941, had allowed Britain $27 billion of credits during the war. The credits allowed Britain to purchase goods from the USA without having to sell it goods in return. As a result, British industry was able to concentrate on war production. The Americans ended the Lend-Lease arrangements as soon as the Pacific War was over, which plunged Britain into difficulties. Exports had fallen by 1944 to 30 per cent of the level of 1938 and manpower and resources could not instantaneously be re-allocated so that Britain could again pay its way in the world. Billions in wartime debt also worsened Britain's position and the sale of overseas assets to help pay for the war had reduced the country's income. An agreement with the USA was essential: most of the Lend-Lease debt was written off and a loan of $3.75 billion at 2 per cent interest was provided. Yet the Americans did attach conditions. The British had to agree to adhere to the system of fixed exchange rates for the different currencies originally worked out at a meeting at Bretton Woods. The pound sterling was to be convertible into dollars. Britain had no choice but to accept American terms, but MPs and the British public did not like being dictated to. What the Americans saw as facilitating international trade the British saw as a loss of economic independence and an undermining of their economic security.

Americans end Lend-Lease

Fixed exchange rates agreed 1944

Fear of the USSR combined with the sense that the USA was not a reliable friend led Attlee's government to take certain important decisions. In April 1947 it was decided to maintain conscription in peacetime: a year's national service was imposed on 18-year-old boys. The only precedent for this decision was the introduction of conscription in the months immediately preceding the Second World War. Plainly, the government feared that Europe might once again be in a pre-war period. Another indication of the same fear was the signing of a treaty of alliance with France at Dunkirk. There in 1940 France and Britain had gone their separate ways; in 1947 they were

National Service

resolved to co-operate, one day, possibly, against a resurgent Germany, more immediately against the USSR.

The clearest sign of the government's belief that Britain would need to steer a course independent of the USA was its decision to develop its own atomic bomb. Foreign Secretary Bevin was tired of being talked down to by the American Secretary of State, but quite apart from issues of prestige, it made good sense for Britain to have the bomb if the USA could not be relied upon. The British realised that the USSR would possess the bomb before long and they reckoned that by the mid-1950s it would have the capacity to bring about Britain's collapse. If Britain were to be able to resist future Soviet threats, it would have to equip itself with weapons capable of doing unacceptable damage to the USSR.

The beginning of the nuclear arms race

2. The Foundation of the Western Alliance

Britain's moves to assume the leadership of Western Europe against the Soviet Union made even worse the problem of national insolvency. The US loan of 1945 had simply eased the problem, which could be solved only if Britain's costly military commitments overseas could be reduced and its exports increased. In Greece Britain had been assisting the Royalists against the Communists by supplying troops, weapons and gold reserves to prop up the Greek currency, with the aim of stopping the extension of Soviet influence into the Mediterranean. Hugh Dalton, the Chancellor of the Exchequer, demanded that Britain should stop its aid to Greece in the spring of 1947. Even less affordable were Britain's commitments in Germany. As the occupying power in the north-west, Britain was responsible for keeping the people of its zone fed. Dalton complained that effectively Britain was paying reparations to Germany. In Britain bread had to be rationed, as it had not been during the war, so that the Germans could be fed. Britain's loan from the USA was being spent on wheat imports to feed the Germans. This state of affairs was not sustainable.

National insolvency

Britain supplies troops to Greek Royalists

In the course of 1946, the Americans had begun to share the dominant British view about the USSR as an aggressive and expansionist power. When the British announced their decision to end aid to Greece and Turkey at the end of March 1947, President Truman spoke of the necessity of containing or limiting Soviet totalitarianism, which he saw as involved in a global struggle against democracy. The Truman Doctrine, as the policy of containment came to be called, found general acceptance in the USA. Aid was given to Greece and Turkey. It was obvious to George Marshall, US Secretary of State in 1947, however, that something more dramatic was necessary if Western Europe was to be revived. In 1947 he worked on his European Recovery Programme, which was announced at Harvard University in June 1947. Ernest Bevin described it as 'one of the greatest speeches in world history'. Essentially, Marshall made an offer of aid. The Europeans were to decide whether to take it and how to use it, though American advisors and specialists would play a significant role in the administration of the funds. The assistance was to be spread across a lengthy period: it was not a disaster fund, but aid for a programme of recovery and growth. Huge sums were involved, eventually around $13 billion. Fearful of Americans bearing gifts and especially of the American will to promote open, not closed economies, the USSR and the Eastern European countries rejected American aid, whereas all the Western states but Spain, following Bevin's enthusiastic lead, accepted it. Hence, the offer of Marshall Aid became a significant factor in consolidating the division of the continent as well as in restoring the prosperity of the Western half.

Restoring the economy of Western Europe was bound up with the controversial issue of the future of Germany. Stalin wanted cast-iron safeguards against future German revenge. He favoured the policy of exacting reparations and de-industrializing the country. Britain came to support a different approach. A policy of crippling Germany would turn it into state which had to depend on the victor-

Britain ends aid to Greece and Turkey

The Truman Doctrine

Marshall's European Recovery Programme June 1947

powers for essential food supplies. It would only cease to be a burden if its economic recovery was fostered. It was also clear, especially to the Americans, that Germany was vital to the whole European economy, revival of which depended upon the recovery of Germany. By mid-1947 the incompatibility of the German policies of what had become the two sides, East and West, was finally destroying what remained of co-operation between them. Britain and the Americans embarked on the process that amalgamated the Western zones of Germany and turned them into the Federal Republic. Plans for a new state composed of the British and American zones were announced in June 1948. In the same month the old currency was withdrawn and a new one, the Deutsche Mark, was issued.

Deutsche Mark issued June 1948

Stalin appreciated that the addition to Western Europe of a West German state would make it far richer and more powerful than the portion of Europe dominated by the Soviet Union. He much preferred to keep the whole of Germany weak and neutral. He could not easily interfere with what the other powers did in their zones, but he thought that he might be able to put pressure on them through their vulnerable sectors of Berlin. Each of the occupying powers controlled a sector of the former German capital, and the western sectors were separated from the western zones of Germany by 100 miles of the Russian zone. In June 1948 Stalin proceeded to cut the rail, road and canal links between the western zones of Germany and the sectors of Berlin controlled by the West. He assumed that the West would be unwilling to appear as the aggressor by forcibly challenging the blockading forces. It might, therefore, be manoeuvred into sacrificing its German plans in return for the reopening of the land routes to Berlin. Alternatively, it might choose to give up its rights in Berlin, which would reveal the West as weak, particularly to the Germans. British officials in Berlin, however, thought up a different way of challenging the blockade. Their idea of an airlift to keep the city going was vigorously urged by Bevin, who saw that Stalin would not want to be the first to resort to force

Stalin blockades Berlin June 1948

by interfering with the airlift. For more than ten months the Royal and United States Air Forces, along with aircraft from the British Dominions, flew into Berlin an average of 4,700 tonnes per day, enough to keep Berliners in food and power. Altogether, more than 200,000 flights were made. In May 1949 Stalin abandoned the blockade. He had not achieved his aims. The creation of West Germany was speeded up, as the French zone joined the other two western zones and the Federal Republic, based in Bonn, came to birth. Stalin had also handed the West a public relations triumph. He had shown himself as dictatorial and brutal and allowed the West to appear humane and generous, especially in the eyes of the Germans.

West Germany created

The crisis over Berlin greatly helped Bevin to achieve his most important objective, the definitive ending of American isolationism and their permanent commitment to the defence of Europe. Unlike earlier British Foreign Secretaries, he had already accepted that Britain could be defended only as part of Western Europe. At the start of 1948, he committed Britain to a Western European Union, a common defence strategy with France and the Benelux countries, but he believed that an effective arrangement to counter the USSR required something bigger to safeguard the security of the North Atlantic area as a whole. Only the USA had wealth and power sufficient to enable Europe to stand up to the Soviet Union. By April 1949 the North Atlantic Treaty Organization (NATO) had been agreed by the USA, Canada and ten European states. This was a remarkable development. Since the time of George Washington, the US had avoided foreign entanglements, but in setting up NATO America agreed to treat an attack on one member as an attack on all. It is not surprising that Congress discussed the obligation of mutual defence for three months before finally approving it. Americans still hoped that having kick-started European defence arrangements, they might soon be able to walk away again. They still did not have large numbers of troops in

North Atlantic Treaty Organization (NATO)

Europe: only two divisions out of fourteen stationed in Europe were American. NATO was a turning point in European history not only because of the still fragile American commitment, but also because of the unprecedented degree of international co-operation that it represented. An integrated Allied command in peacetime was an unheard-of departure from all past practice. The European states and America had come to co-operate in defence, just as the offer of Marshall Aid had produced economic co-operation. This co-operation, reckoned by Stalin to be impossible, was an important reason why the Soviet dictator was not able to call the shots in Europe.

When NATO was founded in 1949, Ernest Bevin had not yet achieved the firm and lasting commitment from America that he sought, but he had gone far in the direction of relieving Britain of primary responsibility for the defence of Europe. Britain was much less overstretched than it had been in 1947. Even though its Empire had shrunk with the withdrawal from Palestine and the Indian sub-continent, Britain might still be able to function as a world power. Such, at any rate, was the expectation of many of Britain's rulers.

3. The Korean War and its Effects

Mao proclaims the People's Republic of China

In October 1949 Mao Zedong proclaimed the foundation of the People's Republic of China after winning a long civil war against the Nationalists under Chiang Kai-shek, who fled to the island of Taiwan. The most important question for the West was whether China would now become a Soviet satellite. Mao had already announced that China should ally 'with the Soviet Union…and with the proletariat and broad masses of the people in all other countries, and form an international united front…We must lean to one side.' He was attracted to the Soviet side by his faith that the Bolshevik Revolution of 1917 and the Stalinist transformation of Russia in the 1930s provided a suitable blueprint for the transformation of China that he intended to initiate. He was also repelled by the Americans, who had supported Chiang and might try to help him recover his power on the mainland. It was therefore not long before American Secretary of State Dean Acheson concluded that Mao's 'Chinese government is really a tool of Russian Imperialism'. Bevin did not agree with Acheson. He was anxious to have good relations with China in order to safeguard the British colony of Hong Kong and British trading interests in the country. He argued that the best way to minimise Stalin's influence in China was to establish Western contacts with it. Accordingly, Britain recognized Mao's Communist regime as the legitimate government of China, whereas the Americans refused to do so. The practical result was that the Chinese Nationalists of Taiwan continued to occupy China's seat in the United Nations Security Council.

Britain recognizes Communist China

The year after Mao's takeover in China a crisis broke out in Korea. The country had been part of the Japanese Empire. When Japan collapsed in 1945, the Red Army found itself in control in the north of the country while the Americans were in occupation in the south. The Soviets and the Americans agreed that the country should be temporarily divided at the 38th parallel until an all-Korean government could be set up and the occupation forces withdrawn. In 1949-50 the occupying troops were withdrawn, but no agreement about the government of the country could be reached. In the south there was an American-backed government created after an election sanctioned by the United Nations. In the north an unelected Soviet-backed government held sway. Both governments claimed to be the legitimate government of the whole country and threatened to enforce their claims by invasion of their opponent's territory. Yet neither could act without the support of its superpower backer.

Korea divided at the 38th parallel

American strategy in Asia was to concentrate on the defence of island strong points, such as Japan and the Philippines, and the US refused to back an attempt by the South Korean President Syngman Rhee to unite Korea under him. Kim Il-sung in the north was no more successful in securing Stalin's backing until 1950, when the Soviet dictator changed his policy. He decided that the Americans were unlikely to intervene and that the danger to the USSR of a war launched by a proxy was minimal in any case. He probably felt that he needed a success to compensate for his failures in Europe and for American success in drawing Japan into their orbit. The permission given to Kim Il-sung to go ahead with his invasion turned out to be one of Stalin's greatest errors.

When Kim Il-sung's forces invaded the south of Korea, the shock to American policy-makers was profound. They did not care about South Korea in itself, but its invasion across a border sanctioned by the United Nations reminded everyone of the aggressions of Mussolini and Hitler. Truman had no doubt that he must defeat the challenge to international order. 'We can't let the UN down,' he repeatedly told his advisors. Within hours of receiving the news of the invasion, the USA had decided to come to the aid of South Korea on the authority of the United Nations. What Stalin had overlooked was that the USA was well placed to come to South Korea's help. It had an army nearby occupying Japan. Moreover, Stalin had withdrawn his representative at the UN in protest at the refusal to accept the Chinese Communists. Hence, the Americans were able to secure the backing of the Security Council of the UN safe from a Soviet veto. Equally unwilling to repeat the mistakes of the 1930s, the British government threw its support behind President Truman and sent both naval and ground forces. Temporarily, the Labour Party united behind its government's policy.

At first, the North Koreans achieved overwhelming success, throwing back their enemies to the south-east corner of the Korean peninsula. The Americans recovered the initiative when General MacArthur surprised the North Koreans by an amphibious landing at Inchon, near Seoul, in mid-September 1950. The North Korean army soon found itself trapped in the south, which enabled MacArthur to advance unopposed into North Korea. MacArthur was too successful for the liking of the Chinese Communists. From October onwards, huge numbers of 'volunteers' crossed the Korean

Margin notes:

Kim Il-sung invades south of Korea

USA comes to South Korea's aid

North Korea's early successes

frontier and MacArthur's forces were driven back. Truman spoke incautiously about a possible use of the atomic bomb. There was consternation among America's allies, not least in London. Attlee invited himself to Washington in December 1950 in order to exercise a restraining influence. Truman gave only vague promises, but he appeared to take enough notice for British policy-makers to reassure themselves that Britain was not just one of the queue of European countries, but 'one of the two world powers outside Russia'.

The Korean War, then, remained a limited conflict. Realizing that this would mean a stalemate in Korea, MacArthur challenged Truman's policy and was sacked for his pains. The British role in the war was a considerable one. Over 90,000 British troops served there at some point in the three-year conflict, many of them National Service men. In the most notable British engagement of the war, 600 'Glorious Glosters' took on 30,000 Chinese at the Imjin River. Most of them ended up dead or prisoners. Total British losses amounted to 1,078, compared with 37,000 Americans. Quite large numbers were taken prisoner and were notoriously subjected to political re-education, popularly called brainwashing. Complex negotiations over prisoners caused the indecisive war to drag on as long as it did. The frontier between North and South Korea ended up more or less where it had been when the war began. It was a small result for the loss of perhaps a million and a half Chinese and North Koreans and a million South Korean soldiers and civilians.

> British role
> in Korea

The effects of Kim Il-sung's invasion of South Korea were even more far-reaching outside the Korean peninsula than they were within it. The Americans and Western Europeans at once supposed that East Germany would next attempt the equivalent of what Kim was attempting, that with Soviet backing it would proceed to invade its West German neighbour. Walter Ulbricht, ruler of East Germany, even boasted that West Germany would be the next to fall. The Americans realized how poorly prepared they were against this eventuality. Since August 1949 they had lost their nuclear monopoly,

USSR a nuclear power

American rearmament

when the Soviets had successfully exploded an atom bomb in Kazakhstan, but on the ground in Western Europe the Western Allies were outnumbered 12:1 by Soviet forces. It seemed vital to the Americans, therefore, to undertake a huge programme of rearmament. The Korean attack persuaded Congress to agree. Truman declared a National Emergency and the defence budget rose from $15.5 billion in August 1950 to $70 billion sixteen months later. The Americans also requested their NATO allies to increase their defence spending, which soared to a post-war peak by 1951-3.

When Attlee flew to Washington late in 1950, he might perhaps have helped to moderate the American approach to Communist China and North Korea, but he also had to make concessions to the USA. The defence budget for the three years 1951-3 already stood at £3.6 billion, but the Americans had pressed for it to be further increased, perhaps even to £6 billion. Practically all the cabinet thought the latter sum economically impossible, but some concession to the Americans was inevitable. Eventually, a programme of £4.7 billion over the tree years 1951-4 was agreed, but at considerable cost to the unity of the Labour Party. The Americans had a further request to make. It was impossible that the rest of Western Europe should pay to defend West

German rearmament

Germany, without seeking any contribution from that increasingly prosperous country. Yet seeking a West German contribution meant raising the sensitive question of the rearmament of Germany only five years after Europe had been freed from its yoke. This issue the British government was now compelled to face. The government was split on the issue, but the American case was unanswerable and if the Germans were kept firmly under Allied control, so it was argued, their rearmament need not be dangerous.

Thanks to the Korean War, Bevin had achieved what he had been aiming for at least since 1947, a permanent American commitment to Europe. The American pledge of 1950 had been a psychological boost to Europe, but only afterwards did the pledge acquire substance when a Supreme Allied Commander was appointed in the person of General

Eisenhower and Allied military headquarters and administrative facilities were established in Belgium and France. In Britain the USA had acquired air bases where, from 1949, were based B-29 bombers with atomic bombs. NATO had been turned into a proper alliance. This had happened because of the confrontation of the two super-powers, each attributing aggressive plans to the other. The USA expected Stalin to strike at West Germany, though it is now clear that the only state he contemplated attacking was Yugoslavia, ruled by the dissident Communist Tito. Stalin's security services warned him about the colossal American military build-up and he came to think that the Americans must intend to assault his sphere of control in Eastern Europe.

American bases in Europe

The Cold War meant that the USA relieved Britain of the burden of leading the defence of Western Europe, a burden beyond the country's strength. It offered Britain a different role, as America's junior partner in the global struggle against Communism.

Conclusion

The Second World War and the period of Labour rule which followed it constitute a watershed in British history. The war began as the latest in a series of wars about the pretensions of one of the European powers to exercise hegemony over the rest. At the end of the 18th and start of the 19th century, the would-be dominant power had been revolutionary and Napoleonic France. In the early 20th century, it had been the Germany of Kaiser Wilhelm II. After founding his Third Reich in 1933, Adolf Hitler was determined to introduce a New Order in Europe, in which Germany would be master of the continent. By 1939 he had come up against the same obstacle that had thwarted Napoleon and Wilhelm II, the refusal of the other European great powers to allow Europe to be re-modelled without their consent. Since Hitler would not permit Britain and France to exercise a veto over the development of his policy, war broke out in 1939 between Germany on one side and France and Britain on the other.

The Second World War did not turn out to be a re-run of the First. The unexpected collapse of France in 1940 changed everything. Britain could not hope to achieve victory on its own and was forced into far greater dependence on the United States than in the First World War. Germany was emboldened to launch an invasion of the Soviet Union in 1941. By the end of 1941 Hitler was at war with the USA and the USSR as well as the British Empire. Though Britain remained one of the Big Three, there was no doubt that it was the least of them. The USA poured out the treasure needed to defeat Hitler; the USSR made the necessary sacrifice of blood. After the war conventional European power politics were not restored, as they had been in 1919. In the era of the Cold War, which began soon after the 'hot war' against Germany had ended, it was the two superpowers which called the shots in Europe. Britain became the subordinate ally of one of them, the United States.

The Second World War differed from the First too in that it came to be about much more than the position of Germany in Europe. The apparent success of the German challenge to the Western powers emboldened Italy and Japan to seek dominance in Africa and the Near East and the Pacific respectively. In effect, they were seeking to be heirs to British power in their respective areas. Hence the challenge to the British Empire was far more direct and serious than any challenges posed to it in the First World War. In the end, these challenges were defeated, but by means that seemed likely to prove fatal to the survival of the Empire. The British had to enlist the help of the USA, which in the Pacific played the major role, but the Americans made no secret of their dislike of European imperialisms. British reliance on Indians and Egyptians increased their disinclination to be drawn into British quarrels and further undermined British dominance in these countries. In the event, after the war Britain was compelled to divest itself of much of its Empire by granting independence to the Indian sub-continent and relinquishing the thankless task of mediating between Jews and Arabs in Palestine. Yet in 1951 Britain still had far-flung imperial possessions, while through the Commonwealth it seemed to possess influence even in many of its former colonies that were now independent. Britain could still persuade itself that it was a world power, despite its withdrawals from places where its position was manifestly untenable. America had turned out not to be as formidable a foe of the Empire as it had originally seemed, because Britain's surviving influence was often useful as the USA squared up to the Soviet Union.

By 1951 Attlee's government seemed able to congratulate itself on having retained for Britain an important and secure place in the world after making certain unavoidable concessions. It seemed also to have established a stable and durable settlement at home. British society was divided by class, but the wartime and Labour governments worked out generally acceptable terms on which the working and middle classes could live together. By 1951 the working classes enjoyed virtually full employment. They were also promised free health care through Bevan's Health Service and security in all those circumstances which in earlier times had reduced working people to poverty, such as accident, disability, ill health and old age. All these benefits were delivered through an enormously expanded state machinery which employed huge numbers of public servants. The *laisser-faire*, small state of Victorian Britain had passed into history. In addition, it was expected that government would be carried on in co-operation with the trade union representatives of working men.

The most notable feature of the elections of 1950 and 1951 was the acceptance by both main parties of all the main features of the post-war settlement established by the governments of 1940-51. Controversy between the main parties was confined to peripheral issues, such as the nationalization of steel, or matters of administrative competence, such as success in remedying the housing shortage. Many of the domestic purposes of government were common ground between the parties. The Conservatives expected consolidation of Labour's achievements to deliver a contented and co-operative working class. Labour was keen on attracting middle-class votes. To that end, it laid less and less emphasis on nationalization and more on the mixed economy. It left the public schools, where many of its ministers had been educated, largely alone. It aimed at and achieved only a very modest redistribution of wealth.

In its period of office Labour aimed to build in England's 'green and pleasant land' a new Jerusalem, where everyone would receive an adequate share of the wealth created by the British economy. It was less concerned with promoting the dynamic growth of the economy and yet without such growth Labour's proud achievements were likely to come under threat. Britain had a unique opportunity in the years immediately after the war to break into the export markets of countries that were still recovering from the war. The opportunity was not taken. Britain continued to depend heavily on old staples such as coal, textiles and steel and there were few signs of new thinking in the City or in the management of industry, while the main concern of most trade unionists was to carry on doing things in traditional ways. It would probably have been impossible for any politicians to change this culture of complacency at a time when Britain had just proved itself in a great war and when the spur of competition from Britain's usual rivals was absent. The Labour government made little effort to change things, despite the series of economic crises in 1947, '49 and '51. A great growth in exports masked the reality that once Britain's economic rivals were back on their feet, the decline of Britain's industrial performance would resume and accelerate. As this happened, the international power which Britain still seemed to exercise in the time of Ernest Bevin would diminish and full employment and generous social security benefits might prove unsustainable.

INDEX

Horton, Max, Admiral 108
housing 159-60
Howard, Ebenezer 164

INDIA: creation of Bangladesh 198;
creation of India and Pakistan 196-8;
Gandhi calls for Britain to quit 194;
Louis Mountbatten appointed Viceroy
195-6; Muslim state of 'Pakistan'
proposed 193; regional governance
189-91, *190-1*; religious and political
tensions 191-5
industry: diversification and
modernization 162; fuel and power
shortages 170; iron and steel 176-7;
Nationalization 153-6, 176-7; strikes
and conflicts 77
IRAQ 186
ITALY: African territories lost 90-3;
campaign in Greece fails 87-8; invasion
by allied forces 104-5; Mussolini
arrested 104; Pact of Steel 1939 22;
Tripartite Pact with Germany and
Japan 128

JAPAN: alliance with Germany 112;
Burma, capture and loss 140-3; capture
of Malaya 132-3; capture of The
Philippines 223-4; capture of The
Philippines 131-2; expansion into
Pacific Islands 134-5; expansion of
territories, map of *126*; fall of
Singapore 133; Hong Kong surrenders
132; invasion of China 125-7; invasion
of Indo-China 129, 134; Neutrality
Pact signed with USSR 128; treatment
of prisoners 135-8; Tripartite Pact with
Germany and Italy 128; unconditional
surrender 148; US drops atom bombs
147; war with United States *130*, 130-
2, 143-6
Jay, Douglas 175
Jews: German anti-semitic policy 16, 112-3;
Palestine, seen as homeland 187, 199-
202
Jinnah, Muhammad Ali 193
Jones, Arthur Creech 203, 204
Joyce, William 83

Kesselring, Albert, Field Marshall 96-7,
104
Kim Il-sung 221-2
Korean War 220-3

Labour Party: associated with working
class 178-9; election defeat 1951 183-4;
election success 1945 152; election
success 1950 177-8; internal disputes
182; party of social reform 150-1; social
reforms 157-8; trade union links 179;
unsustainable spending crisis 170-2
League of Nations 125-6
London Blitz 57, 60, 67-72, *71*
London Passenger Transport Board 153-4
Lynn, Vera 83-4

MacAthur, Douglas, General 132, 145,
222-3
Malaya 132-3, 204
Malta 95, 96-7, 99
Manhattan Project 146
Manstein, Erich von 31-2
Mao Zedong 220-1
Marshall, George, General 101, 118, 217
Mass Observation reports 70, 72, 77
Mediterranean, regional importance 86
middle class and Labour 179-80
mining 77, 155, 156-7
Molotov, Vyacheslav 24, 211
Montgomery, Bernard, General 98-9,
104, 119-20, 122
Moore, Henry 68, *69*, 167
Morrison, Herbert: contribution to war
effort 68, 150; Festival of Britain 1951
165; labour relations 77;
Nationalization, responsible for 153-4,
176; opposition to National Health
Service 158
Mosley, Oswald 84
Mountbatten, Louis 195-6
Munich Conference 1938 17, *18*
Mussolini, Benito 22, 45-6, 87-8, 104-5

National Coal Board 156-7
National Health Service 158
Nationalization 153-6
NATO 207, 219-20
Nehru, Jawaharlal 190, 196

INDEX

Woolton, Frederick, Lord 75, 81-2
working class: government assistance 75-6; Labour Party, association with 178-9
World War II: air superiority, fight for 48-53; Allied bombing of Germany 115-7; Allied invasion of Italy 104-5; Allied invasion of Sicily 101, 104; Battle of Britain 54-6, 58-9; Battle of North Atlantic 106-9; bombing raids on British cities 56-60; campaigns in Greece and Crete 88-90; East African campaigns 90-1; Europe, map of *102-3*; German campaign in USSR 109-12, 113-5; German domination spreads 45; Germans reach Channel 38-43; Japanese aggression and suppression 125-48; Netherlands and Belgium invaded 36-8; North African campaigns 91-101; Norwegian campaign 33, 33-4; Operation Overlord 119-23, *121*; Poland invaded 26-7; Tehran Conference 1943 119; VE Day (Victory in Europe) 149

Yalta Conference 210-1, *211*
Yamamoto, Isoruku, Admiral 130

Zhukov, Georgi, General 111, 113-4